A glance back a

Lydney Docks

Sailing ships loading in the lower docks, circa 1930. A Bristol Channel trading ketch is loading coal from a Lightmoor Colliery wagon at No. 7 tip. Unfortunately none of the vessels are identified, although that on the right is a Severn trow.

by
Neil Parkhouse

Black Dwarf Publications

Acknowledgements

Thanks for assistance and additional information to Greta Wright, Brian Russell, Gwen Richards, Pat Jenkins, Melville Watts, Harold McOwan, Bill Johns, Brian Probert, Neata Welby, Ian Pope, Robin Craig, Colin Green, Roy Fenton, Rick Cox, Roger Carpenter, Mike Meredith-Edwards, S.G. Shepherd, Clive Carter, Thelma Bullen, Barbara Steele and the Welsh Industrial & Maritime Museum.

Owen Hudson, on the right, gives lock keeper Lem Gardiner a hand opening the entrance gates, whilst Lem's daughter Greta (now Greta Wright) watches the photographer. Picture circa 1930.

This book is dedicated to Greta Wright,
in thanks for friendship and for sharing her memories,
and to Brian Russell,
who cares deeply about the docks.

Copyright: Black Dwarf Publications and Neil Parkhouse 2001

British Library Cataloguing-in-Publication Data. A catalogue
record for this book is available from the British Library
ISBN 1 903599 00 8

Black Dwarf Publications
47 – 49 High Street, Lydney, Gloucestershire GL15 5DD

Printed by M.D. Jenkins Ltd.,
Unit 53/54, Lydney Trading Estate, Harbour Road, Lydney, Gloucestershire GL15 4EJ

~ A short history of Lydney Docks ~

For over two thousand years the Forest of Dean has been known as an area of industrial activity, exploited first for its iron ore reserves, then its wood and latterly for coal. Iron ore was mined at the time of the Romans, timber was felled for shipbuilding and charcoal burning up until late Medieval times, and coal was extracted from around 1750. Up until the end of the 19th century, iron making was one of Dean's major industries, along with the manufacture of tinplate. For all these industries, the problem was how to transport their produce to the outside world.

It is likely the Romans first made use of the river at Lydney. Having conquered the local tribes, they used them as manpower in their iron ore mines, workings such as the Scowles which can still be seen today. Whilst the Romans built good roads and made use of them, they were also great sailors and it seems inconceivable that iron produced here, from iron ore mined in the Forest along what is now the Bream road, was not shipped out in some measure by water. It is thought the Severn estuary was much narrower at this time but shortly after the Romans left many of the wetland areas became flooded and it is possible that the sea level may have risen slightly also.

The Severn is a river of tiny inlets and pills, many of which have, over the centuries, provided natural harbours for the communities clustered round them. They led to the development of a distinctive flat bottomed, open-holded vessel which could use them with ease – the Severn trow. The trow could sit on the mud in an inlet when the tide receded and be loaded or unloaded as required, floating off on the top of the next tide; thus wharves and cranes were not required, a warehouse usually sufficing in the way of facilities. This was suitable when loads were relatively small; market goods coming in, and timber and iron going out were the usual cargoes from the Forest.

Although it is likely that Lydney Pill had been a place of shipment since the time of the Romans, it is only much later that the first documented evidence of its use appears. Court

Map of the River Severn at Lydney c1785, based on an original held in Gloucester Library. The formation of the New Grounds had the effect of lengthening the bottom end of Lydney Pill, whilst the top end of it had been shortened by silting. Thus the pill appeared to have moved east, away from Lower Forge works and the church. The notes with the map indicated that the pill was then $1^1/_2$ miles long and that '4 *vessels belong here, one trow for the Severn and three small sloops which trade to Bristol etc.*' The customs observation post was on Nass Point. These posts were manned on a rota, each officer having to cover several points.

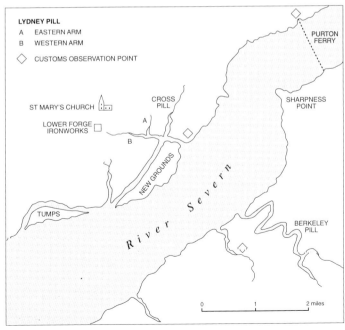

LYDNEY PILL
A   EASTERN ARM
B   WESTERN ARM
◇   CUSTOMS OBSERVATION POINT

ST MARY'S CHURCH
LOWER FORGE IRONWORKS
TUMPS
NEW GROUNDS
CROSS PILL
River Severn
PURTON FERRY
SHARPNESS POINT
BERKELEY PILL

0   1   2 miles

records show a Lydney-based boat trading in stolen timber and venison in 1270, whilst in 1282 another six vessels were reported carrying timber, again stolen. The destination for this contraband was usually Bristol, which for centuries was the main centre of trade for the lower Severn ports. Lydney was also a customs collection point mentioned in a list of 1347.

At this time, the course of the river at Lydney was quite different to how it is today. Contemporary accounts talk of ships being built alongside St. Mary's church and the Severn flowing within sight of it, the river then swinging round in a tight bend to flow round Nass Point. It is likely that the top end of the tidal Lydney Pill reached to within a couple of hundred yards of the church, probably, looking at the lie of the land, to near where the entrance to the Watts factory is today. The two rows of three-storey houses near the station were built just after 1800, on the site of an old warehouse at the pill, so the head must have been quite close to this point. Shipbuilding activities would have been carried on at the end of the pill, so indeed quite close to the church. In the 17th century several large sailing vessels were built here, including two wooden frigates, *Forester*, and *Princess*, the latter being in excess of 600 tons, so a fair depth of water would have been needed at the top of the tide to launch the completed ships and sail them off down the estuary. However, Daniel Furzer, builder of these large warships, wrote in 1664 that '*Lydney is not so fit a place now for building a ship as formerly, on account of the growing of the sands, not known in man's memory before.*' Between 1657 and 1849, it is known that six trows were built at Lydney but it is quite possible other small vessels were completed too.

One of the few features actually named on the original of the 1785 map is the New Grounds, which, as the name implies, had only recently been formed. A gradual receding of the water level in the hundred years prior, coupled with silt being deposited by both Lydney and Cross Pills probably onto an existing mudbank, formed this new piece of land. In turn, this led to Lydney Pill silting up and the navigable channel on that side of the river being squeezed, so by the end of the 18th century it was probably only accessible by quite small vessels, of maybe 20 tons maximum.

Rudimentary routes existed through the Forest, traversed by trains of packhorses but they were somewhat tortuous and prone to the vagaries of the weather. Iron, and later tinplate and coal, were transported in this way, in panniers slung across the animals' backs, but the tonnages which could be carried were naturally small. The Forest terrain and few parish roads not being suitable for carts or waggons, once coal and iron started being produced in large quantities better transport was required.

Elsewhere, from the middle of the 18th century, canals began to be constructed to transport goods to and from inland sites but in the Dean, again due to the nature of the ground, that generally was not possible, although two small canals were built – one at Cinderford, short in length, obscure and short lived, and Pidcock's Canal at Lydney, which needs to be considered briefly because it had a bearing on the development of the docks.

In the early 17th century, the route of the Cannop or Newerne Brook down the valley to Lydney was taken over by the charcoal iron industry. The establishment of Upper, Middle and Lower Forges at various points along its way was all about the abundant supply of water, locally produced charcoal and iron ore mined in the Forest. There only remained the problem of transporting the finished product. Whilst some of the iron was undoubtedly used locally, the rest of it would have been shipped out via Lydney Pill. It is known, for instance, that 80 tons of iron per annum were being shipped to a Bristol merchant by an agreement of 1714, whilst a lease of Lydney Ironworks in 1723 also permitted the use of a warehouse at the pill. In 1790, the various works along the brook were leased by the Pidcock family, makers of fine glass, from Staffordshire. Shortly after taking over the lease, they built a canal connecting Upper Forge with Lower Forge and the head of Lydney Pill. Pidcock's Canal, sometimes referred to as 'The Cut', was wide enough for tubs – small,

A view taken in 1945 from the footbridge by the church, showing a passenger train bound for Lydney Town. Pidcock's Canal is on the right, with the towpath to its right. The canal crosses under the railway at this point. The bridge from which the picture was taken still stands but tree growth has obscured much of the view today.

oblong vessels, which could carry a couple of tons of iron or coal each, and which were pulled along the narrow channel by horses. It was referred to in an inventory of 1844 as '*a navigable canal and locks leading up to the Upper Forge*.' An 1852 map which shows the full length of the canal is unfortunately unclear on the whereabouts of the locks but it is likely there was one at New Mills and another at Middle Forge at least. The canal historian Charles Hadfield believed there may have been three locks, all below Middle Forge. The main line of the Severn & Wye tramroad crossed the canal by means of a drawbridge near Lower Forge and there were further such bridges carrying branches of the tramroad at Middle Forge and New Mills. In 1887, some 9,400 tons of coal and iron were transported between Upper Forge, the colliery at New Mills (Norchard) and Lower Forge, and it is likely that most (if not all) of this was on the canal, the tramroad by this date having been superseded by the railway. The canal was abandoned soon after, however, when around 1890 the works up the valley were closed and production concentrated on Lower Forge. Despite having been out of use for well over a century, much of the canal is still in water today.

For the western side of the Forest, there were two natural outlets for Forest coal – Lydbrook on the Wye to the north and Lydney on the Severn to the south. The Wye is full of shallows and it is a tortuous journey from Lydbrook to the river's mouth. The journey upwards was better and the city of Hereford was the main destination for coal leaving the Forest by the northern route. Ross and Monmouth were also supplied. The Severn, however, is much more suited to shipping.

It was the building of the Forest of Dean tramroad, from Cinderford Bridge to Bullo Pill, and the Severn & Wye tramroad, from Lydbrook down to Lydney, which led to the establishment of new harbours. Proper dock facilities were to be provided at both locations. Meanwhile Gatcombe, which was a busy little port handling timber, iron ore and general goods but which sat at the bottom of a steep drop down to the river, lost out, its trade soon dwindling away to Lydney and Bullo. The first proposals, from the noted canal engineer Benjamin Outram, for a tramroad linking the Severn and the Wye, were presented in 1801. He suggested a harbour at Jack's Pill, near Lydney. In 1806, the eminent civil engineer John Rennie produced a report, suggesting the harbour should be at Nass Point and noting that a basin would be required due to the river being silted up and to protect vessels from the tides. The final survey, by Astley Bowdler in 1808, was very similar to Rennie's and became the basis for the Parliamentary Act, although it did not include an estimate for the construction of a proper harbour. However, Bowdler proved not to be up to the task of construction and was replaced by Josias Jessop but he too did not last long, the S&W wanting a resident engineer and appointing Thomas Sheasby to the post in 1811.

The Act for the Lydney and Lidbrook Railway, dated 10 June 1809, provided for the building of a line from Lidbrook[*sic*] to Lower Forge, Lydney. Although referred to as a railway, this was to be what we consider today a tramroad, with cast iron plates fixed to stone sleeper blocks and waggons drawn by horses. Richard Trevithick had run his steam locomotive on the Merthyr Tramroad five years earlier but Stephenson's *Rocket* was still twenty years away and it was to be several decades before the Severn & Wye converted to a railway. The Act said nothing about the construction of a dock but did mention the provision of suitable wharves on land owned by the Hon. Charles Bathurst.

However, knowing the pill was unsuitable for the level of traffic envisaged, a further Act was obtained on 21 June 1810. It allowed the company to vary parts of their proposed route but more importantly to construct a canal and basin to connect with the River Severn at Nass Point. It is perhaps worth mentioning, in view of local controversy, that 'Nass' not 'Naas', is historically the correct speiling. The latter is an incorrect derivation from sometime in the last 150 years. It may have originated with the crews of sailing ships trading to Ireland with Lydney coal – where Naas is a place name – or perhaps from a misinterpretation of the local pronunciation, which places the emphasis on the 'a', making it sound 'aa'.

In accordance with the new dock works, the Act also provided for the proprietors to change the name to The Severn & Wye Railway & Canal Company. The details of the tramroad do not concern us here but those relating to the dock and canal do. The Act was quite specific: '*by making, completing and maintaining a further Railway or Tram Road … along the Western Side of Part of the Creek called Lydney Pill, down to … Cross Pill, … a Branch of Railway or Tram Road from the said Main Line … across the Eastern Branch of Lydney Pill … to or near to the said Cross Pill; and also to make and maintain a basin … Forty Yards at least above the said Cross Pill, and not exceeding Two Hundred Yards in Length, and Fifty Yards in Breadth, and Twenty-one Feet Deep, to be formed partly from the said Lydney Pill, and partly by excavation and addition … and also to make and maintain a Cut or Canal, not exceeding Twenty-one Feet Deep, Eight Yards in Width at the Bottom, and Twenty-eight Yards at the Top, to extend from the said Basin, and to communicate with the River Severn at a place called Nass Point … with Towing Paths, Mounds, or Banks on the Sides of the said Canal; and also to make and maintain a Lock between the Canal and outer Harbour, not exceeding Twenty-one Feet in Width, and Ninety Feet in length; and also an outer Harbour, not exceeding Twenty-eight Feet in Depth, Eighty Yards in Length, and Twenty-six Yards in Width at the Bottom, with a Pair of Gates, or with a Lock, to open into the River Severn with the Tide…*'.

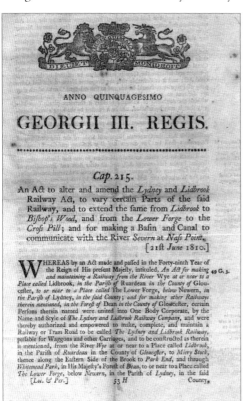

Front page of the Severn & Wye's 1810 Act.

Charles Bathurst, on whose land the upper basin was to be built, also owned the works and collieries at Upper, Middle and Lower Forges and New Mills. Consequently, the Act also stipulated that the lessees of these concerns, both present – the Pidcocks and George Homfray – and future, were to be allowed to use the docks free of any tolls, provision being made for land at the basin to be allotted as a wharf. To this day, this part of the upper basin, from where iron (and later tinplate) from the forges was shipped, is known as the Free Wharf.

Bathurst was also to be paid wharfage dues of £500 pounds a year; any shortfall on this the S&W company had to make up. Compensation, in the sum of £100 pounds an acre plus an annuity of £150, was to be paid to Roynon Jones the elder and Roynon Jones the younger, owners of Nass House and surrounds, for land utilised for the canal and to cover for '*the expected Nuisance or Annoyance to the Remaining Part of their Estate*'. A Swivel (swing) bridge was to be provided for them, so their cattle could reach the grazing land which would be otherwise cut off by the new canal, whilst the Act also recorded their right to fish in the new waterway!

Coal and iron, brought down on Pidcock's Canal, had been shipped from the pill for a number of years but more coal started to arrive once the tramroad opened, this all being shipped from a temporary wharf whilst construction of the dock proper began. A pair of lock gates were provided at the entrance to the canal but a shortage of funds meant the outer harbour was not proceded with. A fair length of canal had thus to be negotiated before vessels reached the new docks, which were opened on 17 March 1813. The *Hereford Journal* recorded that '*five decorated boats, with passengers entered with the flood tide … The bed of the lock is parallel with low water in the river; height of tide in the lock was 23 feet and in the canal and basin 13 feet, which is enough to admit brigs of 300 tons.*' Another vessel came over from Berkeley Pill. The various wharves at the new basin were rented out to traders, who could thus build up stocks without having to pay wharfage. There were cranes for loading and unloading, with the whole being overseen from a dock office building, which still survives today. It is estimated that the new harbour and canal cost in the region of £20,000 to construct and overall the S&W were some £10,000 in debt.

Trade was further boosted when the outer harbour was finally built, being completed in 1821. The tramroad was extended down to it along the north bank of the canal, a branch crossing over by means of the swing bridge which the Roynon Jones' had demanded, to serve tips on the south side of the basin. A further Act had to be raised, however, to pay compensating royalties to Charles Bathurst, whose wharves at the top of the canal soon lost business to those at the new basin. Two new commodities attracted by the improved facilities were china clay, back-loaded from south Cornish ports by coastal schooners instead of ballast, and salt. A moveable stage to facilitate unloading was built for the china clay, which was stored in a newly built warehouse, then loaded into up-river trows for onward shipment to the Potteries. This trade had finished, however, by the mid 1840s. The salt came down from Droitwich in small trows known as 'wich barges' and was stored in a specially built warehouse at the outer harbour but this trade too petered out in the mid to late 1840s. The coal traffic, which from the outset was hampered by a duty imposed on it, was itself boosted when the Duty Acts were repealed in 1833.

The new harbour quickly established itself, the S&W permitting a gratuity to masters of vessels sailing to Chepstow, Newport and Bristol in order to build the new markets. Within a few years, a pattern of Bristol Channel ports and harbours regularly traded to had built up, which continued well into the 20th century and meant Lydney folk often had closer connections with people living in places like Bridgwater and Barnstaple than they did with the next door villages of Aylburton and Blakeney. Over the years, a number of Lydney girls married men off the boats, moving to Somerset or north Devon with their new husbands. Even today, the connection with these places is still remembered.

A portion of an 1824 map which shows the completed harbour. The New Grounds, referred to as the Marsh on the map, is interesting because the landward edge of it probably closely aligns to the previous course of the river at this point. This indicates how short Lydney Pill had been and also how the new canal was cut alongside it. Across the Severn at Sharpness Point can be seen the entrance to the recently constructed Gloucester & Berkeley canal. It was originally intended to reach the river at Berkeley Pill but it was later decided that Sharpness Point was better, possibly because it saved 2 miles of canal and cut costs.

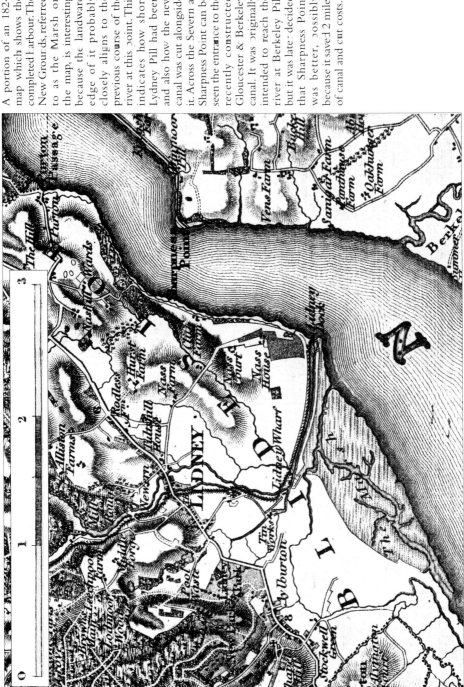

~ 8 ~

The difficulties of navigating into the harbour – there was only a half hour window at the top of the tide for vessels to arrive and leave, whilst ships of 12 foot draught could only reach Lydney on a spring tide – forced the S&W to instigate measures to assist vessels using the port. Fixed beacons were placed on the rocks in Barnacle Channel in 1821 and the company purchased a 6-oar tug boat to pull departing craft out into the river, as well as licensing and paying the pilots. The north pier was also extended in 1825 to aid ships using the harbour. The opening of the Gloucester & Berkeley Canal in the following year, allowing direct passage for large vessels to the docks at Gloucester, perhaps further focused the minds of the S&W directors, for plans were soon being drawn up for a new harbour entrance at Grange Pill, a couple of miles downstream. This would have meant the construction of an even longer stretch of canal but the scheme was not proceeded with because of cost.

The docks enjoyed a busy life throughout the 19th century, both basins regularly being crowded with waiting and loading ships, such that it was often possible to walk from one side to the other across the decks. On hot summer days, waiting vessels would bob gently at anchor, whilst those being loaded would roll as another waggon load of coal was tipped into them, the dust billowing into the air and sticking to the sweat on the arms and faces of the men. The creaking of wooden vessels was lost in a cacophany of sound, as waggon wheels clattered along tram rails, coal crashed into boat holds and men shouted to one another. In the winter it could be an inhospitable place to work, biting cold winds whipping up the estuary and with little shelter from rain or snow. And at night it could be worse, with hardly any lighting and even dangerous if one of the thick Severn fogs rolled in. There was little choice, however; unnecessary time spent in harbour was money being lost, so vessels were turned around as quickly as possible and the short tidal window meant boats had to leave with the tide whatever time of day or night it was. So the docks worked round the clock and this remained the case up until the end of the coal trade, although cargoes were much more intermittent by then.

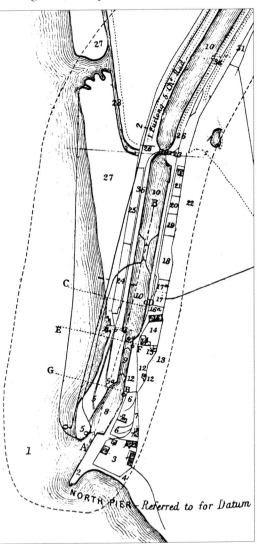

Blackwell's 1852 plan for enlarging the outer harbour.

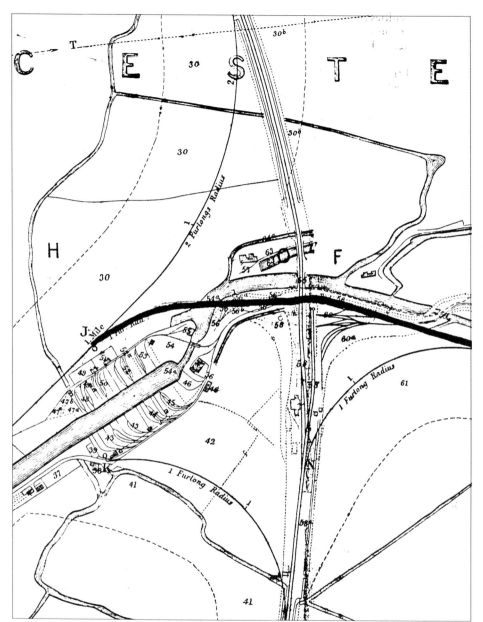

Lydney harbour, upper basin, as shown on Blackwell's 1852 survey map for converting the Severn & Wye tramroad into a railway. The detail is very fine and the purpose of certain lines not at all clear but it appears there may have been as many as 20 coal tips. The thick black line is the proposed S&W railway route. The broad gauge line of the South Wales Railway, opened in 1851, runs across it. Interestingly, this map indicates branches off this line to both sides of the docks, the one on the south (top of map) side being shown running right down to the outer basin. Blackwell's survey was actually prepared at the time the SWR was being built and these branches were never constructed.

This historic view of Lydney Junction station, looking north towards Gloucester, is thought to date from around April 1872 and provides a comparison with the map, left. Later that year, the broad gauge lines were converted to standard gauge. The Newerne or Cannop brook, which had fed Lydney Pill, runs under the railway into the top end of the upper basin. Just behind the photographer were a pair of wooden bridges, crossing Pidcock's Canal and the tramroad which had been laid to connect Lower Forge ironworks with the transshipment warehouse on the Free Wharf. The S&W line to the docks crosses the South Wales Railway mainline on the level in the centre of the picture. Lydney Crossing signal box now stands on the left, whilst the track under the railway is still accessible.

Despite Pidcock's Canal and various streams flowing into it, the S&W struggled for years to maintain the water level in the harbour and also to keep it and the entrance gates clear of silt. Initially, they were periodically cleared of mud by the simple expedient of draining them completely and digging it out with shovels and wheelbarrows. Trade obviously came to a halt when this operation was in progress, which would take at least a week, so in 1847 the S&W began hiring a dredger to clear the canal. This was replaced with a steam dredger purchased by the company in 1879, a similar vessel having already been provided in 1871 to maintain the bed of the outer harbour. In 1890 two steam pumps were finally put into operation pumping water from the river back into the outer harbour.

In 1852, Thomas Blackwell, a Bristol engineer acting as a consultant to the S&W, produced a survey for the conversion of the tramroad into a railway. Whilst this was not acted upon (it was not until 1868 that the conversion was effected), the plans he produced provide a valuable insight into the docks at this time. They also show a proposed major enlargement of the outer harbour which, by virtue of realigning the shoreline and moving the lock further up the canal, would have allowed for a basin seven or eight times the size of that built. Trade at Lydney was severely hampered by the fact that nothing over 300 tons could access the canal, whilst the limit on vessels using the outer basin was 400 tons. The lock into the canal, however, would have been narrower, restricting the upper basin to smaller vessels. The improvements suggested were never acted upon and Lydney remained a restricted little dock throughout its working life but it is interesting to speculate as to whether it may still have been in use today if Blackwell's plans had been carried out.

The plan also shows the tramroad layout at the outer harbour, with the line over the

Another glimpse of the early days is provided in this remarkable photograph of a crash which occurred at the Junction station on Saturday 19 April 1862. The view is looking towards Chepstow and a broad gauge goods train can be seen in the left background, waiting to pass the scene of the accident. On the right are the tramroad tips on the railway interchange wharf. This is about where the fenced railway maintenance compound now is at the present day station. Here, coal brought down in tramroad waggons – it was to be another six years before the S&W itself was converted to a railway, although locomotives were used on the tramway from 1864 – was tipped into waiting broad gauge railway trucks. From its opening in 1851, the railway provided an outlet for Forest coal, initially towards Gloucester and then to South Wales. From 1879 a further route was established with the opening of the Severn Bridge across to Sharpness and then in 1880 the Severn Tunnel opened, providing a direct link with Bristol. Despite all this additional competition for the coal trade, however, the tonnage of coal shipped out from Lydney Docks continued to increase.

The cause of the accident was not fully ascertained. The locomotive involved, *Leopard*, one of Daniel Gooch's 'Fire Fly' class, was itself a singularly unlucky machine. Built in 1840, in 1857 her boiler exploded at Bristol, although nothing is known of the consequences. Rebuilt at Swindon in 1859, she then came to grief here at Lydney. Engine and tender turned on their side and two of the train of three carriages were flung across the down line, out of sight to the left. Only the first class carriage remained on the rails. One of the carriages struck the corner of the goods shed (seen on the right of the line in the view on the previous page) and as a result a Mr. Samuel Bennett, described as a tea merchant of Bath, aged 58 or 59, was killed. At the inquest it was stated that he was thrown from the carriage, as indeed were a number of other injured passengers, being found lying on the ground, with two bad head wounds and one of his legs having been cut off. He was conscious but died in the waiting room shortly afterwards. Ironically, his journey to Cardiff, in the company of his housekeeper, had been undertaken, so it was said in court, for the benefit of his health. The driver and fireman of the locomotive were also injured, suffering burns, scalding and other injuries. It was stated in court that the deceased had complained to the guard of the excessive shaking of the train but was told everything was in order. He thought about changing to first class but baulked at the expense, a descision which cost him his life. It was thought the uneven nature of the main line through Lydney had caused the accident but Gooch and an engineer called Owen gave evidence that this was not the case. They suggested the cause may have been that the front axle of the locomotive had broken. The jury recommended, however, that the company should '*take measures to prevent apprehensions by passengers of the safety of express trains in passing Lydney*' and the S&W duly authorised the SWR to raise the level of the tramroad crossing by a foot. Even today, heavy freight trains still 'bounce' as they speed over the level crossing at Lydney station.

The earliest known illustration of Lydney Docks, a wood engraving which appeared in Mr and Mrs Hall's *The Book of South Wales, The Wye and The Coast*, published in 1861. At the time, the unknown artist producing the illustrations for this book decided that the coal barges were the 'sole peculiarity' at Lydney worth sketching – and we should be glad for that! The sloop on the right would have traded to smaller harbours such as Minehead or Dunster, whilst the trow on the left would likely have been Bridgwater bound, or possibly north Devon. A couple of topsail schooners can be seen in the background of this busy scene, which would have been representative of how the harbour looked for much of the 19th century. There were tramroad tips both sides of the basin, which up-ended the waggons and tipped the coal into waiting boats. Inset: Lydney coal advertisement, 1840s.

swing bridge appearing to serve two coal tips at the basin. There were a number of sidings on the north side, where the clay and salt warehouses were established and where there were also limekilns and a boat yard. Here also had grown the dock village, with homes for the lock keeper, a number of the dock workers and their families, and later a shop too. By 1867, despite the restrictions on larger vessels, Lydney was handling around 200,000 tons of trade a year, mainly coal, pig iron, bark, timber and paving stone. Further plans for improving and enlarging the harbour were deposited by the S&W in 1861 but the company's old General Manager G.W. Keeling, writing in 1910, indicated that the scheme was withdrawn due to opposition from colliery proprietors and traders in the Forest, which seems very surprising.

Major changes came when the S&W was finally converted into a broad gauge railway (the South Wales line it crossed was broad gauge) and new mechanical tips, capable of handling the bigger and heavier railway wagons, replaced the old wooden tramroad tips. Within a few short years, in 1872, the broad gauge line between Gloucester and Newport, which had been quickly absorbed by the GWR after its opening, was converted to standard gauge. The lines of the Severn & Wye company and the Forest of Dean Branch into the Forest from Bullo, also had to be converted. The number of coal tips had been rationalised but each tip could handle more wagons than in tramroad days. There were nine tips, supplemented by three cranes and by the end of the 19th century, Lydney was shipping out around 300,000 tons of coal a year. This might not sound a lot by today's standards but in terms of ships it represents around 2,500 vessels calling in the coal trade alone.

The chart below gives a picture of Lydney's coal trade in the latter part of the 19th century. Forest coal was good house coal and the markets supplied tended to reflect that. Tehidy Manor, home of the Bassett family, mining entrepreneurs of Redruth, was supplied with Lydney house coal up until the First World War, via the tiny and hazardous harbour at Portreath. And whilst over half the tonnage shipped went to Bridgwater,

ANALYSIS OF COAL SHIPPED AT LYDNEY 1881-2

BRIDGWATER★	142,705	ILFRACOMBE	894
BRISTOL★	47,205	MILFORD (incl. Pembroke)	279
BARNSTAPLE (incl. Fremington)	16,808	PADSTOW	342
BIDEFORD	9,431	PORTREATH	2,280
BUDE	270	PENRYN	115
BLEADON	230	PENZANCE	170
BOSCASTLE	360	PEMBROKE DOCK	73
CORK	3,511	PAR	1,004
CALSTOCK	300	PORTHALLON★	105
CHEPSTOW	20	PORT ISAAC	60
CALDY	60	PORT LEVEN★	330
DEVORAN	1,250	TENBY	510
DOVER	170	TRURO	647
FALMOUTH	2,103	WATERFORD	225
FLATHOLM★	165	WADEBRIDGE	3,403
HAYLE	9,175	TOTAL	244,200

★ Bridgwater includes Watchet & Dunball.

★ Bristol includes Weston, Pill & Clevedon.

★ Writing illegible on original list so Flatholm is a guess. It had a lighthouse and was used for sheep pasture so may have required a small coal supply.

★ Writing deciphered as this but no such place. May refer to Porthmellin (Mullion)

★ Presumably refers to Porthleven

courtesy of the big shippers and coal merchants there Sully & Co., Chepstow managed just one tiny boat load, because most of its supply was arriving by rail. Sully's connection with Lydney was such that they maintained an office at the docks and some of their vessels carried Forest names, like the ketch *Parkend*.

Further competition arrived in 1879 with the opening of the Severn Bridge, which provided access for Forest coal to the newly opened dock at Sharpness, the company soon changing its name to the Severn & Wye & Severn Bridge Railway. The S&W built a coal tip there, the new dock enjoying the advantage over Lydney in ease of access as it boasted at least 6 feet more depth of water but still the Forest port continued to grow busier.

Towards the end of the 19th century sail began to give way to steam in the coasting trade, although Lydney continued to be one of the small harbours still visited by sailing boats right up until the early 1950s. Vessels of the Bain fleet, operating out of Portreath, were regular callers, as was the *Ailsa* of Falmouth and numerous other ships taking coal to Cornwall, whilst local JP William Jones ran a fleet of small ships from the harbour, such as the *Forester*, the *Queenstown* and the *Black Dwarf*. Most of their names are now long forgotten but there were hundreds of small ships which over the decades were regular callers.

In common with many small railway concerns, the S&W staggered along for years, its fortunes closely tied with the ups and downs of the iron and coal trades. Luck finally ran out for the directors in the 1890s, however, and the company was effectively bankrupt in 1893. The mineral wealth of the Forest was its saviour, although both the GWR and the Midland Railway fought shy of taking on the debt ridden and run down S&W on their own. Accordingly, a joint agreement was reached and by an Act of 17 August 1894, the GWR and MR purchased the company, each taking an equal share. Further changes of ownership occurred in later years, with the MR becoming a constituent part of the London

This well known late 19th century view shows the upper basin in its heyday, with the canal a forest of ship masts and the dockside a hotch-potch of merchandise. Barrels of cement and crates of general goods are stacked against the wall of the dock office, the gas lamp hinting at the round-the-clock working necessary at the docks; ships had to be loaded to leave on the tide, whatever the time. No's 1 and 2 coal tips can be seen on the left beyond the horse. A steamship, probably the *Black Dwarf*, is moored to the wharf.

Plans were drawn up in 1940 to develop a new industrial estate alongside the docks. Much of it did actually come to fruition but this artist's impression of how the docks would look in the future was sadly not to be. Modern coasting vessels such as that seen on the left were never to visit the harbour and the years after the war saw a quick decline in the fortunes of Lydney Docks.

Midland & Scottish Railway in 1923, followed by Nationalisation of the railways in 1948 but even in British Railways days it was still referred to as the Severn & Wye Joint line.

All of this had little effect on the day to day operations at the docks. Trainloads of coal continued to arrive at the Junction, the rows of wagons then being shunted down to the docks and lined up in sidings awaiting tipping into ships. The bold liveries of the various collieries and merchants painted on the sides of the wagons provided a contrast to their dirty cargo: PARKEND, LIGHTMOOR, TRAFALGAR and CANNOP were a few examples. Boxes of tinplate continued to be delivered to the warehouse at the Free Wharf, brought down from Lower Forge on flat tram waggons pulled by horses. Loaded on the *Black Dwarf*, they were shipped to Avonmouth for onward distribution all over the world, whilst the coaster back-loaded general goods for her return trip to Lydney. This often included 'special' items, with one local woman recalling how, as a girl, she scanned the estuary with a pair of fieldglasses, looking for the tell-tale smudge of smoke that would indicate the tiny steamer was nearly home: "*It might be carrying a great 'hand' of bananas or some other luxury from Bristol; it was only on those occasions that we ever saw bananas.*"

After 1918, however, the great run down started. Coal production, like many other things, had risen to support the war effort but afterwards the need for coal dropped substantially. This led to political unrest, as owners attempted to put miners on short time and short pay and the national strikes of 1921 and 1926 had further drastic effects on production. Closures amongst the big Forest collieries began in the 1920s, with Trafalgar going in 1925, Flour Mill in 1928, Crump Meadow in 1929 and Foxes Bridge in 1930. A new power station was opened next to Norchard pit in 1923, the two being connected by conveyor so coal could be fed directly in. In 1927, the two tips at the top of the canal, used by smaller vessels, were closed and dismantled, and thereafter it was mainly the tinplate traffic which kept the upper basin in use and by 1940 that had dwindled away too.

The Second World War brought another resurgence of activity, with the coal trade picking up again somewhat and the establishment of Pine End works, making the plywood used in the manufacture of Mosquito fighter/bombers. A concrete gantry with crane atop was erected over a new unloading wharf part way up the canal and dumb barges laden with logs were towed by steam tugs up from Avonmouth. Always a tricky harbour entrance to navigate, the sight of a tug with its train of two or three barges manoeuvring through the dock gates at the top of the tide was something to behold and called for the highest

The harbour master's house seen here in the late 1960s after its final occupants had departed. It remained boarded up for years, finally being demolished in the 1980s, a sad loss as it would still have made a fine home but British Rail refused to sell it. In the late 19th century, Captain Samuel Kingscote Lewis was the harbour master in residence here; he was the grandfather of local authoress Barbara Steele.

standards of seamanship. The traffic continued right into the 1970s, and the dock and canal were often crowded with barges waiting to be unloaded or to be towed back to Bristol. A railway branch had been laid down to the works when it opened, an extension of one of the sidings by Cookson Terrace but this closed along with the rest of the railway at the docks when the coal trade finished in October 1960, the last load being shipped out aboard the MV *Yarra*. The Pine End traffic transferred from water to road in 1977, although there was a brief attempt to return it to waterborne in 1986, the last load being brought in by Captain Peter Herbert. Now in his late seventies and still working, he is undoubtedly the last of the old Severn and Bristol Channel sailing skippers still at sea.

And so the story ends. For the last fifteen years the docks have slowly decayed whilst a decision is awaited on their future. An abortive attempt to turn it into some sort of up-market marina, complete with expensive housing, which was most inappropriate and should never have been given planning approval anyway, foundered on the rocks of the house price collapse of the early 1990s but it left the ownership of the site in limbo for a number of years. Responsibility for the docks had gone from British Railways to the Docks Executive and back again, although they were both departments of the British Transport Commission anyway. After closure it was eventually passed to the care of Severn Trent, although not before one final act of vandalism when the old harbour master's house was demolished after British Rail refused to sell it. The old dock village had already gone, although happily the building which incorporated the shop has survived, being used as the headquarters of Lydney Yacht Club for the last few years. And the occasional ship still calls. The MV *Balmoral* does one or two trips picking up from Lydney pier every year. If you are really lucky and the tides are right, it can be an out and back trip but usually its down channel and a coach return from Clevedon on the Somerset coast or Penarth in South Wales. At such times, however, a flavour of the old days is evident.

For the last few years, the ownership of the docks has been vested in the Environment Agency who, after the previous debacle, have not tried to sell it but did briefly consider closing it. Vociferous local opposition, combined with the fact that an Act of Parliament is required to close it, soon scuppered that and attention was diverted to restoration. The lower end and outer harbour have since been listed by English Heritage and plans are slowly coming to fruition to effect repairs, which will cost a lot of money, and to establish a marina. Press notices in 2001 talked of a £1.9m revitalisation scheme by the Environment

Front cover of Lydney guide c1946, the artistic impression of the outer harbour illustrating how closely the town identified with its docks.

Agency and by September it was being announced that the Lottery Heritage Fund had agreed a grant of £873,000 towards that. Once restoration is complete, the EA will be looking to pass the management of the site on to the newly formed Lydney Docks Partnership, which includes representatives of the already mentioned bodies, plus the local councils and also the likes of British Waterways and the Gloucestershire Development Agency.

Plans have been drawn up for a 50-berth marina, a chandlery and workshops, an interpretation centre and cafe, and improved access and parking. As yet, however, because the site falls outside of the EA's flood prevention scheme for Lydney, there is no suggestion of any housing there. A permanent presence is vital, otherwise vandalism will undo any good work done and thieves will descend on the workshops and cafe. Nor is there any suggestion as yet of any heritage development of the site. A reproduction coal tip ought to be a priority, and a length of railway line for possible rides is also worth consideration, whilst more use could be made of the dock shop building, which dates back to the 1820s.

Work is scheduled to be completed by 2004. Quite how many of the 50 berths in the marina will be taken up remains to be seen. This is one of the most dangerous stretches of river in the country (if not the world) which may well discourage all but the hardiest for a start off and who is going to want to leave their expensive yacht/cabin cruiser at this remote location if they cannot live close by to keep an eye on it? Without wishing to be too negative about a scheme we all want to see succeed, there is a feeling that more thought yet needs to go into it but if those involved get it right, it will be a tremendous and exciting asset for the area.

There is also a suggestion of a sustainable energy centre along the banks of the canal, exploring various ways of generating energy by wind and water power. All very laudable perhaps but a row of large white propellors on columns is not in keeping with any heritage aspect of the docks and there are many who shrink in horror at the thought of such desecration of this beautiful site. What it should be is a place that local people can be proud of once more and which both tourists and locals want to visit. There is an opportunity here to create something unique and worthwhile, and the possibility of some commercial traffic should also be considered. A connection with Gloucester Docks and the National Waterways Museum could be forged, with round trips between Lydney and Gloucester utilising both the river and the Sharpness Canal. What needs to be remembered, by all involved – which has been forgotten more than once in recent years – is how deeply embedded in the local psyche are the docks. For over 150 years, they were Lydney's point of contact with the wider world and the affection in which they are held should not be treated lightly.

Lydney tinplate works, or Lower Forge works, seen in an aerial view of 1951, still busy at this stage although closure was only 5 years away. In the background, Lydney Junction yard is full of wagons, long rakes of empty coal trucks waiting to be taken up to one of the collieries, whilst full ones, on the curve behind the steam from the shunting locomotive, await onward transport up the mainline. In the top right corner can be seen the upper basin of the docks, with lines of loaded trucks waiting to be emptied at Nos. 3 and 4 tips. The dredger is moored in the canal just opposite.

The road entrance to the upper basin around 1910, with the dock office prominent. The building survives in industrial use today, although somewhat altered and having been re-rendered and given replacement windows, but it can only be viewed from the Free Wharf on the opposite bank.

'The lifeboat to the rescue!' Lydney Carnival, August 1952: June Meek, coxswain, Pat Meek, bo'son; Claris Roberts, Eileen Brasnal, Wendy Harvey, Elizabeth Biddle, Pamela Perrett, June Boothby, crew; Norman Harvey, shipwrecked sailor. The float was built by lock keeper Lem Gardiner and most of the 'crew' lived at Cookson Terrace, behind. This was built in 1859 by the S&W and named after its then chairman Joseph Cookson. Although mainly built as housing, the larger central portion was the Railway Hotel, which closed in the late 1960s, whilst the Dock post office and the offices of several coal factors and the customs were also located here. The terrace faced onto the upper basin and, up until the 1950s, it was railway and dock workers and their families who lived here.

The *Black Dwarf* with steam up, about to leave the Free Wharf with another load of tinplate destined for Bristol. The transfer shed behind still stands, minus its roof, and is worthy of preservation.

The upper dock in the mid 1920s, with the wharves in use by Edwin Jones. He had a sawmill here, bringing in timber for sawing, and a builder's supply yard, on the left, stacked with bricks, pipes and other goods. Jones' Lydney Carrying Company owned the *Black Dwarf*, seen by the steam crane, as well as *The Forester*, a steamer they had had built in 1910, and a small trow, *Industry*, of 29 tons and built at Chepstow in 1871, which had been used to deliver materials during the building of the Severn Bridge. In the background, Sully, Cannop and Norchard wagons are visible in the sidings.

Providing a contrast to the previous busy views, this photograph of the upper basin was taken by the noted Bristol Channel historian Grahame Farr on 28 April 1951. The water in the canal is still and an air of decay hangs over the scene, although the wharves were still just about in use. Beyond the hand crane, which was of 2 tons capacity, is a small store house and just behind that can be made out the remains of No. 1 tip, dismantled in 1927. Most of the dock fabric seen here survives but is part of the Marina Industrial Estate and not accessible.

Looking towards the upper basin from the end of the canal around 1910. The wharf on the right with its attendant wooden warehouse, was also used by Edwin Jones, carriers and builder's merchants. The trading ketch is not identified and there is a trow moored inside of her at the wharf.

The definition of a trow was usually that it was open-holded and flat-bottomed but within that broad outline, appearances could vary considerably and various rigs were also employed. In this circa 1900 view, two ketch rigged trows can be seen loading at the nearer bank, whilst a sloop rigged trow is under the tip on the other side. Cookson Terrace can be seen in the background. The lack of activity suggests this picture may have been taken on a Sunday.

The Docks, Lydney.

The top end of the canal crowded with small coasting ketches in the early years of the 20th century. The building immediately to the left of the rake of Parkend wagons consisted of No. 18 Dock Cottages and Harrisons shop, which operated as a general stores; they were demolished in the early 1970s. Note the nearer coal tip, of the square type originally provided by the S&W. From 1897, they began to be replaced by single upright tips, such as the one just behind, which needed less men to operate them. The ketch on the right is *Stranger*, of 41 tons and registered at Barnstaple, to where she traded with Forest coal and South Wales gravel.

This photograph of the top end of the canal was taken in 1894 and shows a rake of wagons belonging to the Bridgwater coal factors Sully & Co. waiting to be unloaded. They are on the Upper Docks branch of the S&W. The nearer vessel is a trow, *Jane*, built up river at Bridgnorth in 1810. Of 66 tons, at the time of this view she was owned by W. Davies of Saul. A West Country trading ketch is moored in front of her and both vessels are loading coal for Bridgwater. The trow under the tip in the left distance is sitting squat in the water, indicating she has taken most of her load on board.

Above: The *Black Dwarf*, seen puffing gently down the canal around 1930, was a part of the harbour scene for over 40 years. She was a Clyde puffer, a type of boat built for use on the canals in Scotland, many of which found useful lives far from their birthplace. She was completed by an unknown builder in Glasgow in 1866 for Scottish owners. Of 95 tons, she was sold to Ireland in 1873, changed hands there in 1877, came to a Newcastle owner in 1882 and was brought back to Scotland in 1883. William Jones of Lydney bought her in 1890 and re-registered her in Bristol, her fourth port of registry after Glasgow, Cork and Aberdeen. Another puffer remembered as a frequent visitor to the harbour was the *Snowflake*, which loaded Forest coal for Combe Martin, on the north Devon coast.

Right: An aerial view of the upper basin and canal in 1955, by which time the sidings and tips were all out of use. However, the Upper Docks branch had been extended down to Pine End in 1941 and wagons continued to be delivered to the works until closure of that line in 1964. It crosses the road on the left, by the ditch across the field. At the bottom of the picture are some of the ex- US Army Stores buildings, taken over for industrial use after the war.

Above: The Development Association drew up plans on the outbreak of the Second World War for three new industrial estates in the Forest of Dean – at Cinderford, at Coleford and alongside the canal at Lydney. The latter was to be served by the docks, which it was envisaged would be a major outlet for Forest industry, and by a plethora of sidings running off a new connection to the mainline at Lydney Junction. The Ministry of Aircraft Production began construction of Pine End works in early 1940 and the factory went into production in April 1941. During the war, the output was entirely plywood, used initially to build Mosquito fighter/bombers and later for 'Horsa' and 'Hamilcar' Troop Gliders, such as those used in the Arnhem landings. Ironically, considering the nature of the area, most of the timber processed was imported Canadian birch but some locally grown beech was also used. After the war, Pine End went over to producing timber for use in house building, railway vehicles, motor cars, shipbuilding and furniture. The factory employed between 500 and 600 men and women – the numbers fluctuated with demand – and 40% of the plywood made in Britain was produced here. The raw material after the war came chiefly from West Africa, the huge logs being shipped in to Avonmouth docks and then transferred to dumb barges which were towed up the Severn estuary in trains of two or three by tug. The factory also produced decorative veneers, which were much in demand, using large quantities of Sapele and African Mahogany. Logs of home grown Oak, Walnut and Sycamore were also used for veneers, much of this arriving by rail via the Upper Docks branch. 'Hydrobord', used as a shielding material in the atomic power industry, was another product and the company also marketed a wooden flooring under the trade name 'Par-k-ply'. The picture of the works and canal, above, dates from around 1950. A number of barges await unloading, whilst the railway branch is just visible where it enters the works via the gates to the left of the car.

Left: This 1955 aerial view shows the proximity of Pine End works to Nass House, top, just above which can be made out some of the huts of the war-time Prisoner of War camp, some of the inmates of which were put to work at the docks. Railway wagons can be seen alongside the loading dock on one of the two sidings, whilst several coaches are parked in front of the factory waiting to take workers home. Note the huge stack of logs and the length of the gantry for the overhead cranes.

Right: Advert for Lydney plywood from a Forest of Dean Industrial Handbook, circa 1960.

Lydney			
WEATHER and BOIL-PROOF			
BRITISH MADE PLYWOOD			
SPECIFICATION	BONDING	INSPECTOR	BATCH No.
BS.1455 and BS.1088	WBP		
THICKNESS	FACE SPECIES		GRADE
3/16" to 2"	Mahogany		As Required

The Bristol-registered barges *Myrle* and *Swindon* waiting to be unloaded at Pine End wharf, where they were photographed by Grahame Farr on 23 June 1956. As can be seen, they are heavily laden and there was not a lot of freeboard left with which to tackle the often choppy Severn estuary.

Logs being craned out of a barge at the wharf in the early 1950s. Another barge waits alongside and a row of coal wagons can be seen on the canal embankment beyond. Note how open the canal was then; in recent years, nature has been unchecked and much of the canal is now shielded by trees.

By 1960 there were four cranes at the works for unloading the logs and moving them around the site. The gantry, built in 1940 with the works, had two cranes, one of 5 ton capacity and one of 3 tons, and initially these carried out the unloading of the barges and stacked the logs in the yard. After the war, around 1949/50 as heavier logs came to be brought in, a 7 ton crane was provided and later a 10 ton crane was erected as well. The photograph, below, shows the 7 ton crane unloading logs from the back of an ERF flatbed 8-wheeler in the early 1950s. The 10 ton crane can be seen through the gantry, whilst a pair of barges also await unloading. The nearest barge is *Hanham*.

On the left, an unusual view of the 7 ton crane. The operator was German, an ex-Stuka pilot and PoW, called Stepanik. Why he did not return to his native country after the war no-one knew and he committed suicide a few years after these photographs were taken.

Crane operator Jimmy Edmunds had a lucky escape from this mishap around 1970. The bolts on the crane's bearing had come loose, a regular occurrence but this time it had gone unnoticed. With a log in mid lift, the bolts came out and the crane came out of gear. Jimmy automatically dropped the ratchet lever to hold it but the descending boom had already gathered speed as it fell and the ratchet, at just above head height in the cab, exploded, sending shards of metal in all directions. The cab was left looking like a colander but amazingly Jimmy was unscathed. He later found a piece of metal in his coat pocket! The boom missed the lighter and fell into the water. The Pine End tug is manoeuvring the dropped log back to the canal bank.

On Wednesday 11 October 1972, the largest log ever handled at Lydney Docks was delivered to Pine End works. It was African Mahogany, 31 feet in length, 8 feet in diameter and weighed 27 tons. The timber yielded was used for flooring, boat fittings and special external purposes and the log is seen here about to be lifted out of the hold of the lighter. On the left is George Warwick, with Ron Ballinger centre and foreman (log yard) Merv Rudge behind. Standing on the stern of the barge is Bill Winstone, from Chepstow, remembered as being a very accomplished ball room dancer.

This superb drawing by local artist Eric Rice appeared in an early 1950s promotional brochure for Pine End, then operating under the ownership of Factories Direction Ltd. One of the gantry cranes unload; logs from West Africa, delivered by ship to Avonmouth Docks and then transferred to barges for the trip to Lydney. The contract for transporting the logs from Avonmouth was held by Ashmead's of Bristol, who had a fleet of lighters, as well as several tugs which were used to tow the logs up river and into the lower basin. Once there, Pine End's own little tug was used to take the barges up to the log wharf. They once tried to economise by using a tractor to tow the barges but quickly abandoned the idea when it fell in the canal! The second crane stacks logs in the log yard whilst, in the foreground, another lorryload of plywood leaves the factory along Harbour Road. The log traffic finished in 1977, the last load being delivered on Monday 21 March. Mallinson-Denny, the owners of Pine End, were forced to switch to road transport when the shipping company importing the logs started bringing them into London instead of Avonmouth. Ashmead's maintained it had been a marginal operation from the point of view of its financial viability in any case. Eric Rice's work has appeared in a number of publications, notably the HMSO produced *Dean Forest and Wye Valley Forest Park Guide*, which first appeared in the 1950s and has run to several editions since then. His drawings are well liked by Forest folk and in 2001 he published his autobiography, *Across the Yard*.

The larger 5 ton capacity gantry crane is seen in action above, lowering a log into the storage yard in the mid 1950s. The massive concrete gantries were a landmark at the docks until their demolition in 1986 after the log barges had finally ceased. The slightly later view below shows the massive log stack built up in the log yard alongside the gantry. The main pile, as here, was often over 50 feet high.

Right: The 7 ton crane photographed silhouetted against the sky, shortly before it was dismantled in May 1986.

Below: The timber buyer for Pine End was Mr Farrell, seen here measuring a massive Mahogany log to work out how much veneer it would yield. He was actually employed by Glickstein's, the international timber company who supplied Pine End works at the time and was their main buyer, travelling across the world looking for the best timber. He was very well liked by the workforce and held in great respect because of his skill in assessing the value of the veneer a log would produce. On one occasion a large and very fine African Mahogany log was sent to Pine End 'on approval' – a timber dealer was hoping they would be interested in it. On inquiring how much the log was, the company were told £8,000 (a huge sum in the 1950s) and promptly rejected it as being far too expensive. Mr Farrell, however, told the management to hang on until he'd had the chance to measure it up. He estimated there to be £30,000 worth of veneer in the log so the company quickly changed their minds and bought it! He was an Austrian Jew and his wife was an opera singer, and he is remembered as speaking with a rather high pitched voice, which led to a certain amount of mickey taking, although never to his face. He was always respectfully called 'Mr Farrell' by the workers, to the extent that none of them remember his first name.

Three views taken inside the Band Mill at Pine End works. In the top picture, operator Arthur Stinchombe, on the right, is about to pull the lever to start the carriage moving. Gilbert Wilce, behind, has jammed wedges underneath the log to keep it steady and will keep the two halves upright as the cutting proceeds with the use of clamps and more wedges as necessary. This is a fairly small log being cut here but for bigger jobs the guide for the saw blade could go right up out of sight from this view. The

saw blades were 42 feet long. Having performed the first cut, seen nearly complete in the view below left, one half of the log would then be lifted clear by the third man in the team, Bill Johns, using an overhead pulley, as seen below right. The remaining half would then return on the carriage to be cut in half again, a process known, unsurprisingly, as quartering. The other half would then be dropped back onto the carriage by Bill to be quartered as well. Note that some of the pieces seen stacked in the bottom right picture have had their rough sides cut down as well; this was known as a full quarter cut. The machinery seen in use here was some of that installed when the factory was first built. These early 1950s photographs were taken by Lydney newsagent and photographer Howard Harris, following in the footsteps of his father Frank, and the workers were able to buy copies.

These three views show stages in the making of plywood. Logs which were going for veneer were first stripped of their bark, a process carried out by hand using a long-handled implement called a 'dawker'. The smooth surfaced log was then clamped onto one of three peelers, as seen in this first view. As the machine slowly rotated the log, a cutting blade peeled a layer of veneer off it. The untreated logs always had a high moisture content, so the sheets had to be thoroughly dried next, otherwise the plywood would warp if it was left to dry out naturally. The hot air driers were situated in an area in between the peeling room and the gluing room, thus feeding the sheets from one to the other whilst drying them. This space had also been used for a pillbox in the war, for possible defence of the works. It was taken out afterwards and another dryer put in. It is recalled that the dried ply gave off a very acrid smell, Bill Johns remarking that "*It really tickled your nose until you got used to it.*" Next, as shown in the second picture, the peeled ply fed into a guillotining machine which chopped it into sheets. This was referred to by the workers as a 'donker', because of the noise it made as it chopped the wood. There were always more women than men employed at Pine End, a legacy of wartime. When the factory was first established in 1940 the ratio was something like 10 women to 1 man but even in the 1960s and 70s it was something like 5 to 1. One of the many jobs done by women was feeding sheets of veneer into the splicing machines, as seen in the bottom view. Here the chopped sheets were joined edge to edge, with glue, to form standard sized sheets with which to start making up the ply.

Veneer Peeling Machine

Vertical Veneer Slicing Machine

Crossfeed Splicing Machine

In the early 1950s, a promotional leaflet for Pine End works appeared, featuring drawings by well respected local artist Eric Rice. It took the form of a tour around the factory and the sketches contained are reproduced here. The newly arrived logs were first steamed in pits until they were soft enough for peeling. Even so, the knife blades on the peeling machines lasted only a week at the most. The peelers could cut plywood veneers in thicknesses from as little as $1/100$ in. up to $1/4$ in. Decorative veneers were cut on both horizontal and vertical slicing machines, $1/40$ in. thick and, because the appearance was of greater importance, the knives were reground more frequently. The sheets then spent a few minutes going through the driers, the decorative veneers then being guillotined, tied in packs and sent to the stores, whilst the plywood veneers went to the jointing and splicing machines. Here, the jointers prepared the edges and the splicers glued them together. The sheets of veneer in plywood are arranged with the direction of the grain at right angles to the previous layer. A liquid phenloic glue mixture was then applied to each sheet, except the face veneer, from a

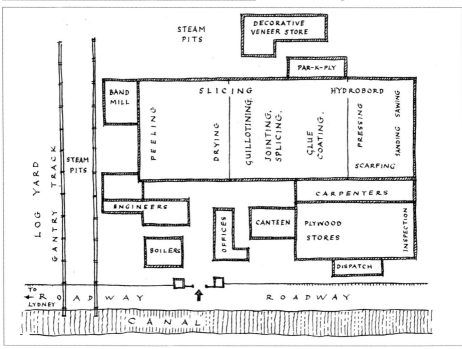

coating machine designed and built by the engineering staff at the factory. Extra thin ply with a book matched face, used in the manufacture of flush doors, was produced using a dry phenolic resin film which was interleaved with the veneers. This was carried out in a different section. The boards then went into the pressing machines, which were hydraulically operated and heated by means of high-pressure hot water circulating through the platens. The temperature was over 100 degrees centigrade and the pressure was in excess of 10 atmospheres, both necessary to set the resin glue. Thicker ply would need up to 30 minutes in the press. The edges of the plywood sheets would then be trimmed by two pairs of tungsten carbide tipped circular saws, before the boards were taken off to be sanded. The sanders could operate at up to 100 feet per minute and the sanding belts needed changing every few hours. The size of the hot press governed the size of board produced. Anything larger had to be achieved by scarfing boards together – the edges of the boards were machine bevelled before being coated with glue and pressed together. There was no wastage from the factory. Trim offs from the sawn plywood were reduced to fragments in a hammer mill and sold for the manufacture of Formwood articles. Wood dust from the various saws, sanders, planers and routers went to a briquetting machine, where it was pressed, without adhesive, into sawdust briquettes suitable for use as a boiler fuel, some of which went to feed the factory's own boilers. The accompanying plan shows the layout of Pine End. It occupied a site of some 14 acres. The manufacture of plywood, as seen here, has long since finished but the factory is still operating as Lydney Products Ltd, making bus and railway carriage interiors, as well as the linings for shipping containers.

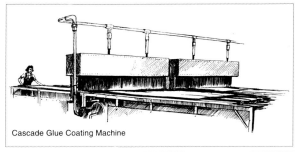

Cascade Glue Coating Machine

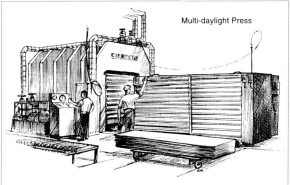

Multi-daylight Press

Wide-belt Sander

Warehouse

Another aerial view of the canal and Pine End works taken in 1955, showing the extent of the factory, part of the ex-US Army Quartermaster Stores base, the swing bridge and Harbour Master's house, No's 6 and 7 coal tips, and some of the old vessels hulked along the river bank to protect it. Note the coal sidings are all empty. The view below dates from around 1930 and shows the swing bridge in some detail, with the HM's house beyond and the dock village and various sailing ships in the distance. The swing bridge had originally been provided for the Jones's of Nass House and had then been used to carry the tramroad across the canal to reach the coal tips at the outer harbour.

Pine End features again on the left of this 1955 aerial view, whilst the lower part of the canal, the lower basin and the outer tidal basin can all be seen The days of sail at Lydney docks had just finished by the time of this photograph and the number of motor ships calling were relatively few, as can be seen by the empty sidings. A few empty log barges by the lock are the only vessels to be seen. All of the infrastructure was still in place however. In the late 1950s the small amount of coal still loaded went out from No. 9 tip in the outer basin. Across the Severn, at the top of the picture, can be seen the piers protecting the entrance to Sharpness docks, busy then and still quite busy today.

The railway enthusiast V.R. Webster paid a visit to the docks in 1939 and snapped this shot of the noticeboard at the swing bridge. All is quiet in the basin but the dredger can be seen moored to the left bank in the distance. Note the bay window and fancy barge boarding to the HM's house, left.

The sign reads:

SEVERN & WYE JOINT RAILWAY
NOTICE
ALL PERSONS OPENING THIS BRIDGE
ARE REQUESTED TO CLOSE & PROPERLY
SECURE IT IMMEDIATELY AFTER THE
VESSELS HAVE PASSED THROUGH

A selection of views of the lower basin, wherein vessels could load at one of three coal tips numbered 6, 7 and 8. These were rebuilt by the Midland Railway around 1909 and, along with No. 9 tip in the outer harbour, in later years saw most of the traffic, simply because they did not involve a trip up the canal. The first view is from the early years of the 20th century and shows the original square, four-posted tips built by the S&W. The second picture is circa 1910 and shows the new tips. It is possible that it was intended to put a fourth tip in this lower basin, because a base was provided – it can be seen just beyond the stern of the small steamer in this view. The wagons belong to Baldwin's, a Bristol-based coal factor. The quieter study below is from the 1950s. On the right is the *Jonadab*, built as a trow at Newport in 1848, rebuilt and decked in 1895, de-rigged and motorised in 1948, and hulked at Lydney in the 1960s.

Above: Another early view, probably around 1905, showing Parkend coal being tipped at No. 7 tip, which is still in its pre-1909 unreconstructed form. A number of Lightmoor wagons are on view; these would have reached the docks via the S&W's Mineral Loop, travelling through Moseley Green tunnel, over Pillowell level crossing and joining the mainline at Tufts Junction for the trip down to Lydney. The vessel is unidentified but is one of the many small West Country trading ketches which called at Lydney.

Right: The schooner *Kathleen & May* alongside No. 6 tip in 1936. She was built at Connah's Quay in 1903 and is now preserved, having recently been completely rebuilt at Bideford. She made her final commercial voyage in 1960, the last fully rigged schooner at work. Behind her is the *M.A. James*, built at Porthmadog in 1900 and hulked at Appledore in 1948. Beyond the swingbridge can be seen the *Garlandstone*, built at Calstock between 1907 and 1910, and now preserved in superb condition at Morwellham Quay on the River Tamar.

The ketch *Progress*, built at Kingsbridge, spent 19 years in the North Atlantic trade, making four return voyages every year to Newfoundland. She is seen here in 1936, long after those halcyon days, loading Eastern United coal probably for Bridgwater or Bristol.

The contents of a Cannop colliery coal wagon being tipped into an unidentified 3-masted schooner at No. 7 tip, around 1930. Note the gas lamp, behind the wagons, to aid night working.

Looking along the roadway leading to the dock village around 1910, with a row of sailing craft awaiting loading moored to the bank. Second along is the *Jane* of Bridgwater, a Mersey flat built at Runcorn in 1800, and the vessel in which Edmund Eglington made his voyage to Lydney harbour *(see inside back cover)*. Very similar in appearance to a trow, she first arrived in the Severn around 1845. She was hulked in 1925 and used for coal storage, and was finally broken up at Lydney in 1939. Edmund Eglinton's famous account (see inside back cover) of a voyage to Lydney was aboard *Jane*. In the view below, a 3-masted schooner and a small ketch wait alongside tips 7 and 8 about 1930; from the lack of activity it would seem likely that both of these views were taken on a Sunday.

The busy view above, taken from alongside the entrance lock into the canal, appeared in the brochure published in 1940 promoting the development of new industrial estates in the Forest. A large schooner is loading coal at No. 8 tip and an ancient looking steam coaster appears on the right. Below, a good profile of No. 7 tip in the 1950s, with a log barge moored alongside and the village in the background.

Although of poor quality, this view is included because it provides a rare glimpse of the original No. 9 tip replaced in the early years of the 20th century. The steamer is not identified but is likely to be bound for one of the Cornish ports. Note how she lies to stern as the aft holds are filled first.

Empty log barges crowd the canal in the 1960s. This view was taken on a Sunday and the barges are waiting to be towed back downstream to Avonmouth the next day. This 'Indian Summer' for the docks ended in 1977 when the timber traffic ceased. In the background is the dock village; the nearer building housed No. 2 Dock Cottages on the far left, No. 1 in the centre and the dock storehouse and workshop on the right. Greta Gardiner (Wright), whose reminiscences appear in the Dock Life section, was born upstairs in No. 2 in 1926; her father Lem Gardiner was the lock keeper. Behind was No 3, the old Lydney Lock House, facing the canal, with a terrace at a right angle to that housing No's 4,5 & 6. In the 1930s, families living here included the Porters, Jim Nelmes, Tosh Nelmes and the Sterrys, with the Organ family in No. 1, next door to the Gardiners.

In the Docks, Lydney.

A busy scene in the outer harbour around 1930, with the small trading ketch *Penryn* in the centre. The crews of the vessels exchange pleasantries as they await tie top of the tide to leave. Of 61 tons and 74 feet in length, *Penryn* was built at Falmouth in 1880 and spent her life in trade from there, surviving as a hulk in the Penryn River until the 1960s. When the lock gates are opened, the boats will make their way out into the channel (many masters refused to pay for a tow) and drift leisurely downstream with the ebbing tide, often not hoisting sail until they reached Beachley.

The outer harbour in April 1952. Under No. 9 tip, loading coal for Ilfracombe gas works, is the 3-masted schooner *Eilian*, a frequent and well-remembered vistor to the docks at this time. She was built at Amlwch, on Anglesey, in 1908 and her varied career in the coasting trade lasted until she was sold to owners in Denmark in 1957. In 1980, she was still at work in the West Indies but has not been heard of since. The two vessels on the left are the MV *Tredegar* and the trow *Edith*.

Long regarded as the most poignant picture ever taken at Lydney docks, the 3-masted schooner *Nellie Fleming* was photographed by Frank Harris leaving the harbour in the mid 1930s. She was lost with all hands (6 men in total) *en route* to Ireland in a great gale in February 1936, whilst outward bound from Lydney with coal and there are many who believe this picture shows her setting off on that fateful voyage. At the end of the north pier can be seen the tug *Resolute*, waiting to help out into the channel any vessels wanting a tow. The *Nellie Fleming* has obviously declined the offer.

A Frank Harris postcard of the 1950s, which shows the *Eilian* under No. 9 tip again. On the left the de-masted and motorised trow *Jonadab* makes another appearance. A frequent visitor to Lydney in the 50s, the river bank outside of the harbour was a fitting place for her to be hulked in the 1960s.

The motorised trow *Emperor* at Lydney in August 1934. She was the last wooden craft to be built at Chepstow, in 1906, and gained her engine in 1920. She was owned by Smith's of Bristol and traded in coal from Lydney until WW2. She was used as a wrecking barge during the salvage of HMS *Warspite* at Mounts Bay in 1948 and ended her life in the 50s when burnt on the beach at Ponsandane, near Penzance.

The tug *Benfleet* in the outer basin in the 1950s. She was owned by Ashmead's of Bristol and was a frequent visitor to Lydney hauling the log barges. Having deposited them in this basin, they were taken on the short journey up the canal by Pine End's own small tug, one at a time as required. *Benfleet* is probably waiting here for some empties to be brought down, to return to Avonmouth.

An unusual aspect of the outer harbour, from above the limekilns in the 1920s. It appears shipwright Alick Gardiner may have just taken delivery of the ship's lifeboat he converted into *Princess Pat*.

The photographer was standing on No. 9 tip to take this tranquil scene, looking across the entrance gates to Sharpness docks, on the far shore, in the mid 1950s. The farther of the two huts still survives today, as does the beacon lamp. When the tide is out, it is possible to walk across to Sharpness, something which the lave net fishermen regularly do but visitors should not attempt this – the tides and areas of quicksand have trapped and claimed a number of unwary folk over the years.

Above: A close-up of the beacon lamp on the north pier.

Right: The massive wooden lock gates in the 1950s, since replaced with metal ones. This view well illustrates the huge tidal range of the Severn at this point – when the tide is in it matches the water level in the harbour. Note the white look-out hut on the left, now demolished.

A rare view from an old glass negative of the coasting collier *Test* at Lydney. This ship had an eventful life; she was built at Dumbarton in 1890 for Belfast owners and carried the unusual name *Number Twelve*. In 1905 she was acquired by Bain & Co., who ran a small fleet of colliers out of the tiny Cornish port of Portreath and boasts their distinctive red 'B' on her funnel. Sold away after WW1, she went through a number of owners before being acquired by Monroe Brothers of Liverpool in

1934, who chartered her to Cunard's, of all people, a year or so later. Repainted in their house colours, she ran a regular service carrying general cargo between Liverpool, the Channel Islands and Le Havre. She was described by one of her masters as being an 'armchair', because she could sail quite comfortably through all sorts of weather and sea conditions. *Test* is seen here at No. 9 tip probably not long after Bain had bought her, loading coal for Portreath for use in the boiler houses of the tin mines around Redruth and Camborne. *Test* was normally used by Bain's on a regular circuit – London to Plymouth with cement, and then empty to Guernsey to load stone for London – but others in the fleet, such as *Plover*, *Panmure*, *Olivia* and *Guardian*, were regular callers at Lydney.

The end of the outer basin showing the lock into the lower basin, with a sailing ship locking through, and part of the dock village, around 1905. The lines on the left lead to No. 9 tip whilst the siding in the foreground, which terminated just alongside the base of the tip, was installed by 1898. It was possibly provided for general goods as it ran along the quay wall but, from its condition, it would appear not to have seen much use. The hut was for use by the shunters and the tip men.

One of the most evocative pictures ever taken at the docks, showing crowds of Lydney people 'promenading' on Easter Sunday 1914. The men are in suits and the ladies in their best coats and bonnets in a picture which vividly illustrates Lydney's love affair with its harbour.

A 2-masted schooner locks up into the canal in the background, whilst under No. 9 tip sits the 325 ton *Ailsa* of Falmouth, waiting to load coal for the mining port of Hayle. She was built by the Ailsa Shipbuilding Company of Troon in 1894. Lydney coal was usually mixed with Welsh steam coal for the boilers of the Cornish mines.

Probably the strangest looking craft at Lydney was the *Nigel*, a noisy beast with a very flat stern. She was a WW1 landing craft, built on the Clyde in 1915 and used in the Dardanelles campaign. After the war she was adapted for cargo carrying and travelled coastwise down Channel and as far as Cornwall, with cargoes of coal and general goods. This might not sound a great feat but when laden she had very little freeboard to spare – fine in the river but not so good out at sea. Mike Meredith-Edwards remembers entering Charlestown harbour with a load of coal and the waves lapping the gunwhales. They were looked at with quizzical amusement by the crew of a Dutch coaster loading china clay, who politely asked "*Is it a U-boat?*" She is seen here attempting to manoeuvre in a crowded outer harbour, under the direction of her captain Sammy Lawrence, in the mid 1930s.

A close up view of the lock, looking towards the river, in the mid 1920s. On the left is Lydney Lock House, originally provided for the lock keeper but later just part of the dock village.

This lovely study of *Black Dwarf* in the outer harbour has only recently come to light. Taken around 1930, the tiny vessel shows the lines of her Scottish ancestry well, as she sits quietly at anchor alongside an unidentified 3-masted schooner. *Black Dwarf*'s register was closed in 1947, after she was broken up, although it is likely her scrapping actually took place some years prior to this.

~ Dock People and Dock Life ~

The first lock keeper was Samuel Hayward, a Littledean man who also carried on a trade as a shoemaker. He was paid the princely sum of 15 shillings a week. The S&W also employed pilots to assist vessels working in and out of the harbour, granting certificates to skilled men from 1823, after one of their number had managed to sink a schooner. Little is known of them but one Richard Sinderby came to be mentioned in the company minute book after he had damaged the outer wall of the harbour by continually running vessels against it, he then compounded his error by being abusive when reprimanded about it by Thomas Sheasby. His annual certificate was not renewed.

Jacob Jenkins was Harbour Master at Lydney in 1837, at the time of his daughter Elizabeth's marriage to John Merrett. Merrett had been born in Berkeley in 1802 but by the date of his marriage was the lock keeper at Lydney, living at Lydney Lock House (this is thought to be the house at the dock village which faced directly onto the lock). John later became the Harbour Master and remained so until his death in 1864, when his body was found floating in the harbour. His wife Elizabeth had died in 1861. They had five children, one of whom, a daughter Mary Ann, is the great grandmother of Thelma Bullen who provided these details from her family's history. Mary Ann married Samuel Clift in 1866, a sailor from Devon, who had sailed deep sea aboard the barque *Gipsy Queen* and coastwise in the ketch *Clara*. This latter was registered at 'Gloster' and he had probably met Mary Ann when sailing into Lydney during his time aboard her. At the time of his marriage, however, he was sailing on the brigantine *Meggey*. Samuel had been married before but his first wife had died of scarlet fever and 11 days later his daughter had died of measles and pneumonia. He eventually left the sea and got a job at the tinplate works. The family lived at Queen Street, Lydney for a while before moving to Middle Forge, where they both died, Mary Ann in 1913 and Samuel in 1922 at the age of 82. His brother George is listed in one census as being assistant Harbour Master. However, in 1881 a George Merrett is listed as living as a lodger at the Albert Inn, Newerne and described as a dock labourer.

Above: Certificates of Character and Discharge for Samuel Clift, relating to his time aboard the ketch *Clara*. He was the bo'sun and was discharged at Hayle on 23 June 1863.

Left: A superb study of the docks dredger, taken in the mid 1920s by the Parkend-based photographer Morton. 'LMS' referred to the craft's owners, the London Midland & Scottish Railway, successors, courtesy of the 1923 Railway Grouping, to the Midland Railway. Standing on the left is Henry Goode, a dock worker; the others are also dock workers and the dredger's crew.

Shipwright Alick Gardiner also opened a general store at the dock village, around 1900, selling groceries, cigarettes and so on, so the crews of ships could stock up on provisions. It is seen, above, shortly after it opened, with Alick on the left and family members posed around. Hannah Jane (Bell) was originally from Yorkshire and Alick had met her when she was working as a nanny at Frampton. It was a large property and the family also had a live-in maid, as Mrs Gardiner was a midwife and spent a lot of her time nursing. Greta Wright, daughter of Lemuel, one of Alick's sons, has fond memories of her grandparents and the shop, although there was the odd scary moment too: "*The worst were some of the sailors off the Irish boats. They would go off drinking for the evening, either up the Railway Hotel, then (1930s) run by Mr and Mrs Green, or right into town, staggering back to the docks at 2 or 3 in the morning. By this time they would be hungry or, if the tide was ready, about to leave and in need of provisions, so would start banging on the doors and windows for food. Grandma would never go down because of the state they were in. Once, one of them picked up a wheelbarrow and threw it through the window! After that, Grandpa made sure there was nothing left loose outside at night. They could be generous as well mind. During the war, when the country was on rationing, we often used to get bacon and fresh butter brought over by the Irish lads.*" The lower picture, taken in the 1920s, shows one of Alick's daughters, Dorothy, playing with her dog Bonzo (named after a popular cartoon dog of the time) outside the shop.

James Galway became Harbour Master after Merrett and he held the position until 1869. Nothing else, at the moment, is known of him. On 14 July 1869, the Severn & Wye appointed James Pick, a pilot from Berkeley, as the new Harbour Master.

A directory for 1885 gives a picture of life at the docks at that time. The harbour master was James Pick, the Dock Post Office (a sub office to Lydney) in Cookson Terrace was looked after by John Harris and the Customs Officer was William Reece, his office also being in Cookson Terrace. Hockaday & Co., coal shippers, and Trevor Powell, coal factors, had offices in Cookson Terrace too, whilst the Railway Hotel there was run by Mrs Emma Ridler. Sully & Co., coal factors of Bridgwater, Somerset, had an office at the upper basin, as did Weedon & Co., coal merchants. Two small shipping companies operated regular carrying services between Lydney and Bristol; Jones & Son advertised that goods could be delivered on Mondays to the docks, their vessel departing for Bristol on Tuesday mornings and unloading Wednesdays. Goods could be delivered to Bristol (City docks) for loading on Thursdays, with the ship returning to Lydney Friday mornings and unloading Saturdays. A complementary service was operated by the Bristol & Lydney Carrying Co., whose vessel ran Bristol – Lydney on Tuesdays and Lydney – Bristol on Fridays. Their agent at the docks was George Jackson. William Jones also had a colour manufactory in premises at the upper basin. Lastly, the ship repair yard alongside the lock was run by William Egglestaff.

James Pick resigned as Harbour Master at the end of 1885. On 15 February 1886, the S&W minuted that Captain Samuel Kingscote Lewis, another pilot, had been selected for the position, which he held until 1910. He had been a captain in the merchant navy and, from 28 May 1880 to 11 January 1889, he was a Bristol Channel pilot. He hailed originally from Purton, near Berkeley, where he was born in 1851. He was the father of a son, James, and three daughters, Hilda (Wild), Rosa (Stock) and Victoria (Yeatman), the latter being local authoress Barbara Steele's mother. He died on 29 January 1915 and is buried in Lydney churchyard. There is a plaque on his grave to his son James, who as First Mate on board a naval ship, was killed in 1918, only a few days before the armistice which ended the First World War.

Grantley Smith was appointed Harbour Master on 20 April 1915 and carried on until the late 1920s. His son Harry also worked at the docks and he had a daughter too, Renee (Bullock). The 1923 directory once more paints a picture of the people and businesses connected with the docks. Kate Hopkins was sub-postmistress at the Dock Post Office and Edward Baynton was resident Customs Officer. A small grocers shop near the upper basin was run by Edwin Harrison, whilst Alick Gardiner, whose main occupation was as the shipwright leasing the repair yard, was listed as keeper of the shop at the lower basin. William Jones had died shortly after the end of the First World War, in which one of his sons was killed. One of his other sons, Edwin, who

Letterhead for Joesph Knight, colliery agent and shipper, and agent for the Dean Forest Coal Company Ltd.

was already trading under the title E. Jones & Son, general merchants, continued with the Lydney Carrying Co., which he had probably been running with his father for many years anyway. Parkend Deep Navigation Collieries Ltd, major shippers of coal through the docks, had an office there and Sully's still had one too. The Dean Forest Coal Company, coal factors, Joseph Knight agent, also had an office. Knight had a half share in a 50 ton Bideford-registered ketch named *Emu*, along with T. Mitchell from Penryn, near Falmouth.

The next Harbour Master was Captain Maclean, a Scotsman. He never married and lived at the HM's house with his two sisters. The Harbour Master after him was a Captain Sear, a Liverpudlian, and then, in the mid 1930s, came Captain Billy Bury, who held the position until the 1950s. Billy Bury was a retired merchant sea captain from Goole, in Yorkshire, who had spent his seafaring days in the North Sea trade, sailing to Scandinavia and Germany. In Hamburg he met the woman who became his wife and she is remembered by older Lydney folk as having a thick German accent. She had a hard time during the war, not from local people but because her large family still lived in Hamburg. Being an important sea port, it was heavily bombed and her family were also all anti Nazi.

A family with a long association with the docks were the Gardiners. Alick took over the lease on the shipyard around 1898 and was still working there in the '30s. He also opened the shop at the lower basin, in the house where the family lived. His wife, Hannah was also a mid-wife. Pat Jenkins (nee Biddle) related how Mrs Gardiner delivered her mother and her six brothers and sisters at Cliff Farm. Years later, Pat's mother recalled being sent to the docks when the birth of another sibling became imminent – *"You knew it would be all right once Mrs Gardiner was there."* Alick's son Lemuel lived in No. 2 Dock Cottages and was the lock keeper at the docks. He had five children, Raymond, Harold, Kenneth, Greta and Graham. Greta was born upstairs in No. 2 in 1926 and her recollections of life growing up at the docks and the other families living there have been invaluable.

"Next door to us at No. 1 lived Reg Organ and his family, who moved over from Berkeley. They had two children, a girl and a boy who both tragically died, the girl from illness, whilst the boy drowned in the harbour. Apparently, he was riding his bike along the path and hit a flagstone at the dockside, flipping him into the water, bike and all. The first anyone knew about it was when they saw his cap floating in the dock. Afterwards, they had two more children, Madeline and Reg. The building on the end of our short row was used as a storehouse and workshop by the dock repair gang. The Sterrys moved into the house facing the lock. They later took over the shop from my grandmother. Mr Sterry worked at the docks, as did his son Bert. They also had a daughter, Doreen. There were two lots of Nelmes and the Porters – Mr Porter operated the crane at the outer basin. In 1937 we moved to a house at the upper basin, No. 18 Dock Cottages, next to Harrison's shop, and Bob and Mair Roberts moved into No. 2 Dock Cottages.

From our point of view as children, the harbour was a wonderful place to grow up. Our grandad, Alick, had a little boat he used to take us out in occasionally, a ship's lifeboat he'd bought and converted and named Princess Pat. *Later our dad, Lem, who was lock keeper at the docks, bought another lifeboat and made it into a little cabin cruiser which he named* Princess Pat 2. *He used to sail her up and down the harbour and we would often join him. We had a small rowing boat too called*

Grace Darling. *I remember one day, when I was about eleven, I was in the hut on the pier with dad when one of the Sharpness pilots came in, needing a lift back across the river. There was no-one available so our dad said 'Greta can take you' and into the rowing boat we jumped. It might seem odd now but I was the only girl in the family and with four brothers I was just treated as another boy. After I'd dropped him off, I started rowing back. I can remember clearly to this day our dad stood on the end of Lydney pier, with his megaphone, shouting instructions to me. He directed me up river, towards the Severn Bridge, until I was able to catch the ebb and float back down*

Alick and various other members of the Gardiner family aboard *Princess Pat* in the early 1930s.

to the dock. Dad caught the boat with a hook as I came alongside the pier. It never happened again. Our mum got to hear about it and went spare – she gave him a right telling off!

It was a beautiful place to live, although it was a fair walk to Lydney Church School which we attended. We used to play with the Biddle children outside school hours, who were similar ages to us and lived just across the field behind. We had to make our own entertainment most of the time, such as swimming in the basin, although looking back the water must have been quite dirty. My brother Harold was always the daredevil and he used to dive in off the top of the coal tip (No. 9). The men off the boats often used to give us little presents like sweets or occasionally bananas, things we would never have seen otherwise. There was a Walls ice cream 'Stop-me-and-buy-one' used to come down the docks in the summer and courtesy of the fishermen, we often had shrimps, elvers or crabs to eat. And we never went short of coal!"

Pat Jenkins, whose family, the Biddles, owned much of the farmland around the docks (Roynon Jones' old estate) had fond memories of the docks too: "*The water in the upper basin used to be bright orange, brought down by the canal from the tinplate works. 'Pickle Brook' we called it. I'm not sure what the stuff was but it was used to 'pickle' the tin, to prevent rust. I can remember swimming in it and afterwards my nails would be a gold colour, which I thought very glamorous! Whatever the chemical was, it did us no harm and the water was a fantastic colour.*

My grandparents owned the land on which Pine End factory and the American Quartermaster base were built – it was compulsorily purchased in 1940. The huge gantry that was erected to unload the massive tree trunks from Africa was a source of wonder to locals when it was first in use. I remember one of the managers, Mr Reissner, from somewhere in central Europe I think, who lived in a bungalow built at the back of the factory. It was made from plywood produced at the works and I remember it being a very attractive home with its wood-panelled rooms. It is now demolished. To the best of my knowledge, the US Army never used the docks."

Gwen Roberts (Richards) was the daughter of Bob and Mair Roberts, who moved into No. 2 after Greta Gardiner's family moved out and she provided a few memories of life at the harbour in the late 1940s/early 1950s:

"*We had no piped water or electricity. Water had to be carried from the pump until 1952, when we were finally connected with a mains supply thanks to the efforts of my father who had pressed for it to be laid on. We collected rain water for use in the outside toilet and lighting was by means of oil lamps. Between the cottage and the Harbour Master's house was Trenchard's garage. The residents used to take their glass jar batteries to him to be re-filled with distilled water, so that they could work their radios. However, the garage burnt down during the early 1950s. Around the same time, I remember a Corona lorry drove into the canal near the factory entrance. This was at a time when many things were still difficult to get and people were wading into the water to retrieve the bottles and fishing*

Pete Klooker operated a small marine engineering business at the docks in the 1920s and 30s, offering a repair and installation service to the motor ships which began to be seen in the harbour more frequently at this time. Below is one of his billheads, relating to the repair of an Irish vessel, the MS *Isaly*, in 1931. Above is a photograph of his wedding, around 1910, to Nellie Gardiner, another

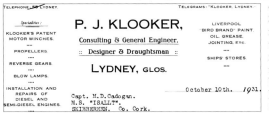

of Alick's daughters. They were married at St. Mary's and returned down to the docks for their reception, where this picture was taken. They then went to live in Pete's native Holland for a while, until he returned to start up his marine engineering business. They are seated 4th and 5th from left, second row and Alick and Hannah are 8th and 9th along the same row.

them out with makeshift nets. It was mostly bottles of Orangeade – anyone finding a different flavour thought they'd got a prize. The water was so muddy you couldn't tell what you'd got until you'd got it out. When they got the lorry out there was nothing left!

I remember the sailing ships still coming in, particularly the Emma Louise *and the* Eilian, *and also the dock being dredged. A diver wearing a large brass helmet and enormous boots would go in the water to help clean the bottom. During the war, American forces were based in a camp at Nass Lane. The GIs would walk down to the docks and chat to my grandfather in the garden, giving him sweets to pass on to us kids. The factory workers would come down in their dinner break too and stop for a chat. One other memory is of a sailor off one of the boats who was called Dick. Quite a character, he would stop and ask for a 'latch opener' – which was enough money to buy himself a pint at The Railway Inn. He would then try to get others in the pub to pay for top ups!"*

Also remembered with affection is the little ship *Black Dwarf* and her crew. An ex-Clyde puffer, she was bought by William Jones mainly to run between Lydney and Bristol carrying tinplate and general goods. Jones was a member of the local gentry, a JP and, in conjunction with his son Edwin, ran the Lydney Carrying Company. Wanting a romantic name for his decidedly unromantic looking little craft, Jones supposedly chose the title of one of his favourite novels, Sir Walter Scott's *The Black Dwarf*. It was certainly apt. Her first skipper was Captain David Davis Goode who died aged 46 and was buried in Lydney churchyard. He left a wife, Sarah, and two children, Christina and Henry. Mate/engineer on the boat was Edwin Hopkins, who died of leukaemia in 1916. He had 8 or 9 children and his widow Kate ran the sub post office at the docks. Jack Tamplin took over as engineer, until the mid 1920s At the age of 60, he had a heart attack and fell into a stream near the golf links, where he drowned in six inches of water. The last captain of the *Black Dwarf* was Floyd Camm, whose family still live in Lydney.

Mike Meredith-Edwards worked down the docks from his early teens, often playing truant to do so. He later sailed on many of the vessels which used the harbour and is now one of the last of the breed. His tales are legion and will one day make a book in their own right. One such concerned one of the old fishermen, Bobby Riggard. There was reputed to be a ghost haunted the docks, an unsurprising rumour given that there was a mortuary there (it still stands – the little brick building next to the limekiln). Lem Gardiner even got in the paper with a tale of it attempting to strangle him. This all preyed on the mind of Bobby Riggard. Down at the docks one night he came upon another of the fishermen, Jim Smith, unlocking his bike which was chained to some machinery near the mortuary. All Bobby saw was Jim's face lit up by his torch, and he put two and two together and came up with five! He took off down the path but Jim, realising what had happened, quickly jumped on his bike and pedalled silently after him dragging the chain. Bobby, who was well over 60, broke into a trot but still the rattling noise got closer. He finally jumped on board his boat and collapsed, and then had a heart attack and had to be rushed to Lydney hospital! He lived to fight again and the story has gone down in the folklore of the docks.

Another well remembered character was 'Mojo', a Rhode Island Red cockerel which belonged to Cap'n Bill, skipper of the de-rigged trow *Willie*. Now the Sterrys, who had moved into the old Gardiner house and taken over the shop, kept some hens there. 'Mojo' could find himself on his travels for two or three weeks, so was then quite eager to get back to Lydney. He seemed to know when

Captain Maclean was Harbour Master in the 1920s. He was what was referred to as a 'four ringer' – a fully qualified ship's master with the four gold rings on his sleeve to show it.

Alick Gardiner, Lydney shipwright for nearly 40 years, pictured around 1930.

A snapshot of the *Black Dwarf* steaming up the canal in 1938.

Floyd Camm, last captain of the *Black Dwarf*, seen here in later years in a sketch by the late Basil Merrett of Lydney.

A motley crew on board the *Nigel*. Despite the noise it made – its Ruston diesel engine had a distinctive chug-chug beat which could be heard halfway down the estuary and it was also blessed with chain operated steering, the vessel was popular with the wives of dock men, who often cadged lifts over to Bristol on her for shopping trips, then returning home by train. The lady here is Marie Gardiner and just to the left of her is the *Nigel*'s skipper Sammy Lawrence.

Marie is also seen again here, standing on the dockside with husband Tom Gardiner in 1924. They never had any children, the lad standing with them being Harold Gardiner, then aged 3, one of Lem's sons and Greta's older brother. The vessel behind loading at No. 9 tip is probably one of the many Cornish steam coasters which regularly called at Lydney to load coal.

approaching the harbour and would be up the bow of the *Willie*, crowing like mad, neck craned into the wind, practically towing the boat home. Before they reached the dock he would have flown ashore, into the pen and serviced 40 or 50 hens before exhaustion, or Mr Sterry, got the better of him.

Captain Billy Bury was the last of the 'four ringers' to hold the post of Harbour Master. After he retired in the 1950s, with the sharp decline in traffic at the docks the post itself became less important and the appointment of time-served ship's masters was deemed unnecessary. Bert Williams was the first ordinary dock man to take on the post which he held until January 1976. Doug Haffenden was the Harbour Master in March 1977, when the log barges stopped coming. He had started work at the docks in 1957, just in time to catch the last of the coal traffic. Employed along with him were two gatemen, Herbert Rowles and Wilf Turner. Then came Dickie Price and Bill Hardy, whilst latterly, in the 1990s, Brian Price was Harbour Master for a while, followed by Chris Hardy. The current holder of the title is Severn Water Bailiff Dave Penfold.

This fearsome looking creature is a sturgeon, which was caught by one of the fishermen, just off the harbour in 1910. On the left is a young Lem Gardiner (Greta's father) and on the right is Alick Gardiner.

Princess Pat 2, an ex-ship's lifeboat converted by Lem Gardiner, motors up the canal past No. 18 Dock Cottages in the early 1950s, with Harold Gardiner at the wheel. She was used as the Gardiner family 'run-a-bout'.

One of the periodic hazards with dock life were the tidal floods, which came about with a certain combination of heavy rain, strong winds and high tide. Not a long lasting flood because most of the water would drain away on the ebb but it still got your feet wet! This is the old shipyard and house under watery siege in 1972.

Brian Russell, staunch campaigner for the preservation of the docks, sitting on the south pier steps. Note the damage caused by tidal erosion, which could cause the wall to fail at any time but which has not yet been repaired. In the 1940s, the level of the foreshore was a foot below the bottom step.

Another recent photograph starkly illustrating the damage done by frost and water incursion to the south pier, which is in imminent danger of collapsing ino the river. The north pier is nearly as bad.

~ Shipbuilding and Shipwrights at Lydney ~

Although not a great ship building centre, a number of vessels were built at Lydney and nearby in the 17th, 18th and 19th centuries. In 1608, two shipwrights and a ship carpenter were recorded as living in Lydney parish. The first recorded constructions were in 1633. Two vessels, one of which was of 70 tons, were built using the King's timber without permission and consequently they were seized by the Admiralty. Nothing else is known of them but they were almost certainly trading vessels, probably trows.

Between 1657 and 1667, Daniel Furzer built three mighty wooden battleships for the King's Navy and a trow of 20 tons at Lydney. One of them, the frigate *Princess*, weighed 620 tons and took two years, from 1658 until 1660, to build. Daniel was later made Surveyor to the Navy. However, the silting up of Lydney Pill curtailed the building of larger vessels and only two small ships, both under 100 tons are recorded as being built in the late 18th century, although a ship carpenter was listed as living at Nass in 1733, so it is likely repairs to trading vessels at least were being carried out.

In 1834, land below David Mushet's wharf at the upper basin was let to David Davies for use as a shipyard. Davies hailed from Sketty, near Swansea. He completed his first ship, *David*, in 1836 and his last, *Try*, in 1864. It is possible some of the later vessels may have been built in conjunction with a William Davies, either a son or brother. Also in 1834, land to the east of the dock entrance was let to Thomas and James Shaw of Gatcombe. No vessels are known to have been built by them here, however, and they were recorded as still building at Gatcombe in 1843. Meanwhile, it was discovered that Davies' operations near the upper basin interfered with the running of the dock and he relinquished his yard in 1835. It is obvious he moved to another site, quite possibly to the yard leased by the Shaws, which is likely to have been that next to the dock entrance. In 1884 a Joseph Brinkworth built a small sloop, *Annie*, at Lydney, possibly at this yard but William Egglestaff is shown as the shipwright in the 1885 directory. In 1892 the yard was taken over by C.W. Dodgin, who came from Bristol. He built at least four vessels here, all of steel construction.

From about 1898-9, the yard was then leased by Alick Gardiner, who carried out all manner of repairs but is not recorded as building any ships. He did, however, adapt and motorise an ex-ship's lifeboat for family use, which he named *Princess Pat*. His son Lemuel (Lem), who became the lock keeper, later bought another lifeboat and converted it to a small cabin cruiser-type craft, also for family use and named *Princess Pat 2*.

The Gardiner family had a long history of boat building and repairs on the River Severn. Around 1830, Ezra Gardiner built a trow called *Spry* at Brimscombe, on the Thames & Severn Canal. Around 1860, his son Benjamin Gardiner was building vessels at Framilode Passage, completing three ketches, *Sarah*, *Hannah* and *Susannah*, and a trow, *Elizabeth*. Whilst it does not relate directly to Lydney, it is interesting to include details of the purchase of one of these vessels – *Sarah*. Her owner/captain took possession of his new craft and sailed her across the river to Broadoak, where he loaded timber for Spain. Having discharged there, he backloaded scrap iron for Plymouth and from there he loaded a cargo for Cardiff. Having discharged once more he then loaded grain for Gloucester, after which he returned to Benjamin and paid him for the ship out of the proceeds of the round trip! In such a way was business done. Benjamin Gardiner had four sons, Walter, Alick, Joseph and Albert. Walter and Alick went into business repairing ships at Lydney, whilst Joseph had a similar business based at Saul Junction on the Gloucester & Berkeley Canal. Alick continued in business at Lydney until the 1930s.

When he finished the yard was left to rot away. Its site and the old slipway is now used by Lydney Yacht Club. In a small way they have carried on the old traditions, carrying out minor repairs and refurbishments to some of their craft on the site of the yard.

A selection of snapshots of vessels under repair on the gridiron – it referred to the arrangement of timbers on which ships needing repair rested when the tide went out. Above is a Wich barge under repair about 1920, a type of trow built for the salt trade from Droitwich. Left, Alick Gardiner, Pete Klooker and some workmen examine the propellor shaft of a steam coaster. It was to handle this sort of job that Klooker set up his workshops, just behind the gridiron, Alick being much more of a wooden ships man.

The ketch *Telegraph* under repair around 1920. Of 70 tons, she was built at Barnstaple in 1869 and had three owners, based at Watchet, Minehead and Braunton, which gives some indication of where she mostly traded to. She was lost in 1923 when she foundered off St. Anns Head, on passage to Wexford with coal from Newport. In this view, she looks to have been pulled a little way up the bank to keep her clear of the tides, so was possibly under lengthy repair.

Even older than *Telegraph* was the ketch *Dispatch*, built in 1852, also at Barnstaple. She was tiny, of 36 tons, and spent her life in the Bristol Channel coasting trade. She is seen here on the gridiron in the early 1920s, probably for some minor repairs to her superstructure. The gridiron was a difficult place to work. Each tide brought a fresh layer of silt, which had to be scraped off the gridiron timbers before any work on the hull could be undertaken. There would be an all too short a window then before the next tide came in.

In 1910, William Jones had had built a small steam coaster, *The Forester*. It was disposed of sometime in the mid 1920s, probably around the time he acquired the 85 ton *Queenstown*, seen here. She was bought in 1925 and her name reflected her Irish origins. She was built by McIlwaine & MacColl of Belfast in 1892, for the Cork, Blackrock & Passage Railway. In 1924, following the amalgamation of the Irish railways, her ownership passed to the Great Southern Railway, based in Dublin but they did not bother to register her. She was sold to William Jones in July 1925 and he re-registered her in Gloucester in September. As can be seen, she was still showing her Cork registration when this picture was taken, which would suggest a date for the photograph of around August 1925. Jones had probably just got her over from Ireland and put her straight on to Gardiner's gridiron for a check up and a spot of refurbishment. She was used on similar duties to *Black Dwarf*, carrying coal, tinplate and general goods, and her register was closed in May 1939, after she was broken up. She was photographed by Morton of Parkend, for whom the docks must have held a fascination, because he is otherwise not known to have strayed out of Parkend with his camera. Alick stands on the left with daughter Dorothy (holding Bonzo) and daughter-in-law Marie on the vessel's stern.

A view of the gridiron about 1910, showing the little rowing boat *Grace Darling* in which, years later, the 11 year-old Greta Gardiner rowed across to Sharpness. Beyond is a glimpse of the late and much lamented Severn Bridge. This picture also gives an indication of what a muddy, slimy place the gridiron was, dangerous to work on unless most of it was cleaned off first.

The Severn Bridge from Lydney.

LIST OF SHIPS KNOWN TO HAVE BEEN BUILT AT LYDNEY

YEAR	NAME	DESCRIPTION	WHERE BUILT	BUILDER
1633	Two ships (one of 70 tons)	seized by Admiralty (*built of King's timber without permission*)		
1657	FORESTER	5th rate frigate, 266tons	Lydney Pill	Daniel Furzer
1657		Trow, 20 tons	Lydney Pill	Daniel Furzer
1660	PRINCESS	4th rate frigate, 620 tons	Lydney Pill	Daniel Furzer
1667	ST. DAVID	4th rate frigate, 646 tons	Cone Pill	Daniel Furzer
1790	HERCULES	Schooner, 91 tons	Lydney Pill	
1794	FORESTER	Sloop, 50 tons	Woolaston Pill	
1836	DAVID	Schooner trow, 54 tons	Lydney harbour	David Davies
1841	FLOWER OF THE SEVERN	Sloop trow	Lydney harbour	David Davies
1841	LADY OF THE FOREST	Schooner, 98 tons	Lydney harbour	David Davies
1842	JOHN	Trow, 30 tons	Lydney harbour	David Davies
1843	SEA SWALLOW	Sloop, 17 tons	Lydney harbour	Davies
1844	ELIZABETH	Trow, 25 tons	Lydney harbour	Davies
1845	FANNY	Sloop, 33 tons	Lydney harbour	Davies
1849	ONWARD	Sloop, 33 tons	Lydney harbour	Davies
1849	LYDNEY PACKET	Dandy sloop, 45 tons	Lydney harbour	Davies
1852	MAID OF BARRY	Sloop, 22 tons	Lydney harbour	Davies
1853	NEW LYDNEY TRADER	Smack, 40 tons	Lydney harbour	Davies
1854	BROTHERS	Sloop, 33 tons	Lydney harbour	Davies
1857	HOTSON	Schooner, 53 tons	Lydney harbour	Davies
1864	MYSTERY	Sloop barge, 30 tons	Lydney harbour	Davies
1864	TRY	Sloop, 28 tons	Lydney harbour	Davies
1884	ANNIE	Sloop, 38 tons	Lydney harbour	Jos. Brinkworth
1895	A1	Screw steamer, 127 grt, 66 net	Lydney harbour	C.W. Dodgin
1895	S&B LTD. NO. 5	Steel barge, 16 tons	Lydney harbour	C.W. Dodgin
1895	S&B LTD. NO. 6	Steel barge, 16 tons	Lydney harbour	C.W.Dodgin
1897	ALPHA	Screw steamer, 33 grt, 5 net	Lydney harbour	C.W. Dodgin

Right: The remains of the shipyard and slipway on 19 April 1952. Only the keels of a few rotting hulks remain. In the background, the Gardiner's old shop and home is still inhabited, and there is a rare glimpse of the mast loft beyond. This is the only building surviving today, in use as the headquarters of Lydney Yacht Club. The building probably dates from c1820, when the outer basin was completed and, as such, is deserving of some proper attention and perhaps better use if the docks are rejuvenated.

The name on this magnificent schooner, sitting proudly on the gridiron at Gardiner's yard, cannot be seen but it may well be the *Kathleen & May* (originally *Lizzie May*) – she traded regularly to Lydney, right up until the mid 1950s. The display of bunting is in celebration of a wedding in the Gardiner family. A gentle breeze has stiffened the flags and the tide is completely out behind.

An interesting postcard view of the early 1950s, showing a motorised barge, possibly the *Jonadab*, and a trow leaving Lydney harbour in tow of the tug *Resolute*. The trow will have been bow-hauled out of the basin by the men standing on the end of the pier, where the tug would have been waiting to pick up the tow. The tide is at its peak and will shortly begin to ebb.

What the river giveth the river taketh away! Ever since the formation of the New Grounds, the Severn has been gradually eroding the river bank at Lydney, along 'The Tack' and the canal bank. The picture above, taken in 1946, shows graphically the effect the tides were having. Lately the problem has got so bad that even the main railway line through Lydney is perceived to be under threat. Consequently, the Environment Agency are now building a new river wall and barrier outside of the harbour, to protect against the erosion of the river bank and to prevent flooding. Over the last couple of decades heavy boulders had been tipped along the bank to stop it receding and previous to this, in the 1950s and 60s, many old sailing craft were hulked along the bank to protect it. Filled with stones, they were beached and left to rot. *Nibley*, seen below in the mid 1950s, was an old Stroudwater barge and many trows, latterly reduced to dumb barges or motorised hulls, ended their days here too. The most notorious was the *Jonadab*, which was hulked in 1963 but floated off on a high tide in the late 1970s, sailing herself across the river and blocking the entrance to Sharpness docks. She was towed back across, beached above the yacht club and some of her timbers broken to ensure she did not repeat the escapade. Although the Severn has done its best to wash the remains of these vessels away completely, the keelsons of some of them can still be seen when the tide is out.

Although not directly connected with Lydney Docks, the loss of the *Rameses II*, in the river just across from the harbour entrance, is well remembered by local folk. She was an Egyptian ship, bound for Sharpness with 7,000 tons of Russian grain on 23 March 1951 (Good Friday), when she grounded on a sandbank. Not knowing the river, the Egyptian crew panicked and were all for launching the boats. Only after a tremendous argument did the pilot manage to persuade them not to and a couple of hours later, with the tide out, they were able to walk ashore. *Rameses II* broke her back on the bank with the weight of her cargo and, being in the navigable channel, presented a serious hazard to shipping. Over 6,000 tons of her cargo were salvaged but the vessel had to be cut up where she sat,

a long drawn out operation which amazingly was not completed until 1960, nine years after she had run aground. In all this time, the wreck had to be lit to warn other vessels using the river at night of her presence. By the end, she had sunk so far into the sand her sides were simply cut down to riverbed level and the rest left, so occasionally, the remains of her keel do still appear at low tide.

Right: Although in very poor condition, this snapshot of the *Mogens Koch* about to enter the harbour in the early 1920s is included because she was an unusual vessel to be calling at Lydney. She was a 4-masted steel auxiliary schooner, built at Svendborg in Sweden in 1919. Of 385 tons and 139 feet in length, she was equipped with a diesel engine, as well as electric lights and a wireless – real mod cons! She was owned by A/S Bornholms and registered at the port of Ronne. She is obviously unladen in this view and, as it would seem highly unlikely that she had come all the way over to Lydney for coal, the most likely scenario is that *Mogens Koch* had delivered a cargo of Baltic timber to Sharpness. She has then come across to Lydney to back-load coal for her return home, although it would also be unusual for her not to have found a cargo at Sharpness.

Left: The motorised trow *Edith*, built at Chepstow by William Hird in 1901, was a regular visitor to the docks and is seen here, at the top of the tide, chugging gently in through the entrance gates, with her coggy boat in tow. *Edith* was motorised quite early, in 1927. Of 44 tons, she was just short of 75 feet in length. Latterly, she was owned by Smith's of Bristol, who ran a fleet of ageing vessels, both sail and steam, with several other trows including *William*, *Alma*, *Spry*, *Superb* and *Emperor*.

Below: This young lad fishing off the remains of the gridiron in the early 1950s seems oblivious to the presence of the motorised iron ketch *Mary Stewart* of Braunton. Built at Montrose in 1876, from 1925–58 she was captained by W. 'Professor' Parkhouse of Braunton, not a known relative of the author, although he too was born in that Devon village. *Mary Stewart* has turned into the still running tide to gain steerage to enter the dock.

Right: Two snapshots which capture the end of an era at Lydney docks – the last trainload of coal to be shipped out on 31 October 1960. The top picture shows the wagons being backed down to No. 9 tip in the charge of an ex- GWR 5700 class tank engine. The young girls posing for the camera are, from the left, Heather Johnson (Woodward), Sylvia Kiely (Nelmes) and Gwen Roberts (Richards). The second view shows the locomotive silhouetted against the sky, standing on the bridge over the sluice.

Below: This photograph provides good detail of the coal tip and its method of operation. It shows the very last wagon load of coal shipped from Lydney being tipped into the MV *Yarra*. The *Yarra* was built at Bristol in 1880 and although classed as a trow, her hull form was described as being more akin to a trading ketch. She spent much of her life in the fleet of captain Alexander Watkins, of Saul, until she was de-rigged and motorised in 1949 – in which condition she is seen here. She later lost her engine and spent her final working years as a dumb barge.

A selection of pictures taken in 1972/3, showing log barges arriving at the harbour in tow of Ashmead's of Bristol's tug *Peter Leigh*. The tug motors past the end of the pier in the top picture. On another occasion, two children watch as it manoeuvres the barges into the dock entrance, as the river exhibits a moment of almost dead calm at the very top of the tide. In the background, a ship leaving Sharpness can be seen slipping down river. The train of barges are then seen entering the basin, past a row of empties waiting to be taken back to Avonmouth. Finally, on a previous occasion, *Peter Leigh* was photographed off the end of the pier as it arrived to pick up some empty barges. This was the last commercial traffic to use the docks, finishing in March 1977. A trial run at starting it again in the mid 1980s came to nothing.

The harbour and even the town of Lydney have been prone to flooding over the years, although these were not regular occurrences. The defence works currently being undertaken by the Environment Agency are designed to alleviate this but the outer basin will still flood on rare occasions if the right (or wrong!) conditions occur together. Heavy rainfall bringing excessive water downstream, meeting a flood tide coming up with a gale force wind behind it will still lead to scenes like this. The top view shows the remains of the dock village under water in 1972, whilst the other two show the outer harbour filled to overflowing around 1953. The entrance gates are open to allow some of the water to drain away with the ebb and a crowd of local people have come down to marvel at the spectacle. Standing on the pier in these conditions, they must have felt almost as though they were marooned on an island!

Lydney Yacht Club have been largely responsible for keeping the harbour alive since the last commercial traffic ceased. Although only a small club – facilities are basic and it is a treacherous stretch of river – the club has managed to keep going for over 30 years and have held regular, well attended regattas. The top view dates from around 1970 and shows some of the yachts belonging to club members, with empty log barges in the foreground. Below is a photograph showing the basin crowded with boats and visitors to one of the regattas in the late 1970s.

The old harbour still enjoys the odd day of excitement and importance when a preserved pleasure cruiser calls to pick up passengers. In the top view, *Balmoral* is moored to the north pier loading trippers for a cruise down channel to north Devon and then to Penarth, from where her passengers will be brought back to Lydney by coach. These trips are normally two or three times a year and on rare occasions, if the tide times are in favour, an out and back trip from Lydney pier is possible. For *Balmoral* cruising in the Severn Estuary is a return to home ground as for a while she had been in the ownership of P & A Campbell until withdrawal in 1980. In the lower view the paddle steamer *Waverley* steams past the end of Lydney pier heading for Sharpness. The last sea-going paddle steamer in operation she makes a wonderful sight on her annual visit to the Severn with occasional trips to Sharpness. Most local people will probably be amazed to learn that she has never visited Lydney, being too large to work in. The last paddle steamer to visit was Campbell's *Ravenswood* in 1893.

The position of the harbour has always meant it was exposed to the extremes of the weather coming up the Bristol Channel and estuary, as graphically illustrated in these two photographs taken on 16 February 1985. The bitterly cold temperatures have frozen the water overflowing the entrance gates, producing a fantastic icicle display. The bottom view is looking at the site of No. 9 tip, which any redevelopment of the docks ought to have scheduled for reinstatement, to properly illustrate what the docks were about. Those working on the dock project will probably, looking at these pictures, be amazed to know that there are many people who would love to live down here, so some well designed housing should be a prime consideration. No one expects the docks to remain frozen in time but left to rot or an ill-thought out development should not be options either. As we await the finalisation of plans, let us hope that Lydney harbour can look forward to a new lease of life.

Bibliography

The Severn & Wye Railway	H.W. Paar.	1963
The Canals of South Wales & the Border	Charles Hadfield	1960
The Last of the Sailing Coasters	Edmund Eglinton	1982
The Westcountrymen. Ketches & Trows of the Bristol Channel	Gordon Mote	1986
Old Time Steam Coasting	Spargo & Thomason	1982
The Victoria History of the County of Gloucester, Vol V. The Forest of Dean	Ed. by N. Herbert.	1996
The Industrial History of Dean	Dr Cyril Hart	1971
Severn Traders	Colin Green	1999
Men of Steel. The History of Richard Thomas and his Family	David Wainwright	1986